SUPER INTELLIGENCE RISING

Blueprints to Turn AI Into Your Growth and Wealth Engine

RAJITHA RUPANI

Author Name: Rajitha Rupani
Author Email Address: contact@rajitharupani.com
Author's website: Rajitharupani.com/book

Super Intelligence Rising, Rajitha Rupani —1st ed.

CERTIFIED

(H)

WRITTEN
BY HUMAN

To every human rising through disruption —
and to every machine learning to serve purpose.

To my sons, for reminding me that strength and softness
can co-exist.

And to those reinventing themselves after the storm —
may this book be your spark to rise again.

CONTENTS

ACKNOWLEDGMENTS

This book was not written in isolation — it was co-created through countless human and agentic collaborations.

To my mentors, peers, and friends who believed in the vision of *Agentic Transformation* long before it had a name — thank you for seeing the light before it became visible.

To my sons, who gave me both the reason and the resilience to keep building. You are my constant source of strength, grounding, and purpose.

To my partner, for your encouragement and presence through this process — thank you for being a quiet anchor while I poured my energy into this vision.

To my sister, who became my content manager, sounding board, and creative co-pilot — thank you for helping bring polish to my ideas when they were sparks on paper.

To my parents, family and friends for their blessings, quiet prayers, and unwavering belief that I could rise through any storm.

To every colleague, customer, and leader who shared insights during this journey — your stories shaped these playbooks.

And to the entire Fhyris community and my network, for supporting this tough journey through your encouraging words, likes, comments, and sharing your stories along — you are proof that reinvention is not a luxury, but a superpower.

PROLOGUE

The Age of Unraveling

Something is breaking, not quietly, but everywhere, all at once.

In boardrooms and factory floors, in government buildings and home offices, a silent tremor runs through the system.

Layoffs roll out in waves, headlines blend into each other, *"Restructuring. Efficiency. AI-driven transformation."*

But behind every press release is a person staring at a screen, wondering what just happened to the job they built a life around.

Governments are debating budgets while algorithms decide fates.

Startups are automating entire departments before they've even built teams. And in the chaos, the world feels suspended, half human, half machine, unsure which side is still steering.

Some of you might have experienced this before.

Every industrial leap has rewritten the story of work, but this one feels different.

This time, intelligence itself, the very thing that defined us, is being reconstructed in code.

And it's happening faster than anyone can comprehend.

—*ⱺⱺⱺ*—

The headlines say it's about AI.

But underneath, it's about *agency.*

Who gets to decide what happens next — humans or the systems we've created?

Who bears responsibility when an algorithm replaces empathy with optimization?

Who leads when every process, every job, every conversation becomes intelligent?

For the first time, technology isn't just executing — it's evolving.

It's learning our behaviors, shaping our decisions, writing our futures.

And as it rises, we are faced with a question that history has never asked this loudly before:

Can humanity keep up with the intelligence it created?

This is the moment of **SuperIntelligence Rising**, when the systems we built begin shaping the systems we become.

———◈◈◈———

This book was born from that question.

Not from theory, but from lived experience — in the middle of economic uncertainty, leadership reshuffles, and cultures unraveling under the pressure to "transform."

Everywhere I looked, organizations were adopting AI faster than they could adapt their people.

Boards celebrated automation wins while quietly asking: *"What happens to the humans?"*

But beneath the fear, I saw something else — an awakening.

Leaders questioning not just efficiency, but purpose.

Teams realizing that success in the next era isn't about scale, it's about *alignment* — between humans and the intelligence now shaping everything they touch.

———◈◈◈———

This is not a book about technology.

It's a book about *designing humanity's response to it.*

Because the real revolution isn't the rise of artificial intelligence — it's the rise of *agentic intelligence:*

Humans and machines acting together, with purpose and accountability.

The companies that thrive next won't be the ones with the biggest models or fastest tools.

They'll be the ones that build systems where intelligence is shared — where people feel empowered, not replaced; where AI doesn't remove meaning but *restores* it.

This isn't a warning.

It's a wake-up call — and a blueprint.

We can't stop what's coming.

But we can decide what it means.

And that decision — how we rise through it — will define the next century.

So, if you've felt the world shifting under your feet — if you've watched headlines blur into anxiety and wondered, *what's my place in all this?*

Then, this book is for you.

It's not about surviving the age of AI.

It's about leading it. Together...

Welcome to the era of SuperIntelligence Rising—an era we are not just entering, but shaping.

INTRODUCTION

Agentic Transformation – Building the Future of Work, Growth and Success with AI

Introduction: Rising Through Transformation

There are moments in life when the ground gives way beneath your feet.

When what you thought was certain dissolves. When you face a storm so fierce that you must decide—collapse under its weight or rise higher than you ever imagined possible.

For me, that storm came in the form of personal upheaval, professional loss, and a reckoning with identity. I had built a reputation on results—leading global teams, scaling new markets, and architecting customer-success programs that touched thousands. Then, like so many of us, the narrative I thought I was writing was abruptly rewritten. Restructuring. Shifts in power. A seat at the table offered—then quietly taken away.

At the same time, my personal world was being rebuilt from ashes: single parenting, a new home, a new life to piece together for my children and myself. I had a choice—shrink, settle, and survive, or rise, reinvent, and lead again.

I chose to rise.

And in that rise, **Fhyris** was born—not just a company, but a philosophy.

A phoenix for the modern era.

A belief that reinvention is not failure; it's the future.

That resilience is not endurance; it's a strategy.

That transformation is not what happens to us—but what we choose to do with the fire.

But this mission is bigger than me.

Because I know I'm not alone.

Every day, there are entrepreneurs, executives, and creators who feel the ground shifting beneath them. There are companies clinging to old playbooks while the world rewrites the rules. There are leaders asking, *"How do I not just survive the age of AI—but thrive in it?"*

This book gives you the answers to some.

Why This Book Exists

We've entered an era where **AI is no longer a tool—it's a partner.**

Where success belongs to those who can orchestrate intelligence: human + machine, vision + data, empathy + precision.

That's what I call **Agentic Transformation**—the shift from passive adoption of technology to active, intentional collaboration with it.

This book is a guide for anyone who wants to turn disruption into advantage. It's not written for theorists; it's written for doers—the builders, leaders, and dreamers designing the next generation of intelligent enterprises and intelligent lives.

What You'll Get From This Book

By the end, you'll walk away with:

- **A new mental model** for thriving in the age of AI and Super intelligence.
- **Field-tested playbooks** to redesign your business, your team, and even your own role through the lens of agency.
- **Practical frameworks** for entrepreneurs, leadership, customer success and digital growth—drawn from two decades of transformation work across industries.
- **Inspiration + action:** real stories, recipes, and ready-to-run systems that you can implement immediately.

If you've ever felt left behind by technology or uncertain how to keep up with its velocity, this book will show you that *you don't have to chase the future—you can design it.*

How to Use This Book

Think of *Agentic Transformation* as both a manifesto and a manual.

You can read it cover-to-cover or dive into the sections that match where you are today.

- **Chapters 1–2** lay the foundation: what "agency" means in an AI-powered world and how we move from automation to intelligence.
- **Chapters 3–6** explore transformation across industries— customer experience, finance, healthcare, and small-business growth.
- **Chapters 7–10** shift inward: building agentic teams, data intelligence, culture, and leadership.
- **Chapters 11–12** bring it all together with the blueprint for designing an Agentic Enterprise.
- **The Recipe Library** turns concepts into action— step-by-step playbooks you can run tomorrow.

Use it as a reference. Highlight, dog-ear, copy prompts, test frameworks.

Treat it like a ***digital-age field guide***—a companion for building systems that think, adapt, and evolve with you.

The Invitation

Whether you're a founder scaling your startup, a corporate leader reimagining your organization, or an individual rebuilding your life after change—this book is for you.

Because the future doesn't belong to those who fear disruption.

It belongs to those who **rise through it**—those who design intelligent systems that amplify human potential.

Welcome to the rise.

Welcome to **Fhyris**.

Welcome to the **Era of the Agentic Enterprise.**

"So what does it actually mean to rise through technology rather than be replaced by it? Let's start with the foundation—the new meaning of agency itself."

CHAPTER 1

The Age of Agency

The rise of humans + AI agents as the foundation of future work and business

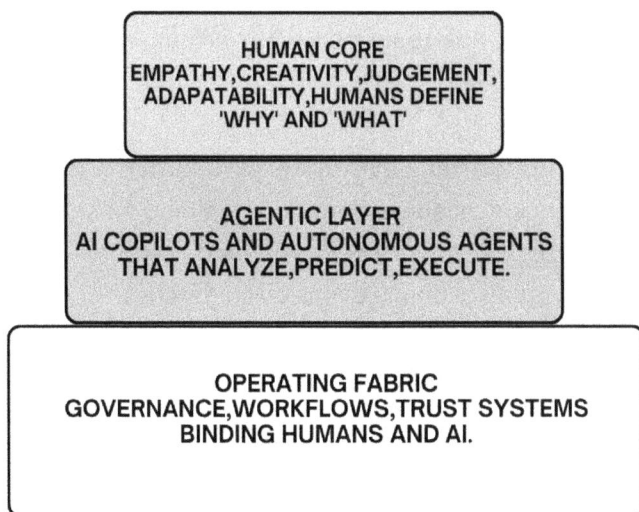

```
┌─────────────────────────────────────┐
│           HUMAN CORE                 │
│  EMPATHY,CREATIVITY,JUDGEMENT,       │
│  ADAPATABILITY,HUMANS DEFINE         │
│       'WHY' AND 'WHAT'               │
└─────────────────────────────────────┘
┌───────────────────────────────────────┐
│           AGENTIC LAYER                │
│  AI COPILOTS AND AUTONOMOUS AGENTS     │
│   THAT ANALYZE,PREDICT,EXECUTE.        │
└───────────────────────────────────────┘
┌─────────────────────────────────────────┐
│          OPERATING FABRIC                │
│  GOVERNANCE,WORKFLOWS,TRUST SYSTEMS      │
│      BINDING HUMANS AND AI.              │
└─────────────────────────────────────────┘
```

For decades, technology has been our tool. It automated the predictable, digitized the analog, and connected the world. But automation and digitization were never the destination, they were only the warm-up act. Today, we stand at the dawn of a new era—one where humans and AI agents operate side by side, not as master and machine, but as collaborators shaping the next chapter of business and work.

This isn't science fiction. It's already here—woven into our workflows, customer experiences, and everyday decisions. The resilient human spirit is now paired with adaptive intelligence. And those who learn to orchestrate this harmony—between human and machine—will define what comes next.

The Shift That Changes Everything

Every revolution has reshaped what it means to act, decide, and create.

- The **Industrial Revolution** gave humans the power to produce at scale—machines amplified muscle.
- The **Digital Revolution** amplified memory—computers extended our ability to store and process.
- The **Internet Revolution** amplified reach—networks connected people and ideas globally.

But this moment is different. It's not about amplifying what humans already do. It's about creating partners in action—intelligent counterparts that can reason, learn, and evolve alongside us.

That shift changes everything:

- How work is done.
- How organizations scale.
- How leaders lead.

Success will no longer come from working harder or even knowing more—it will come from designing ecosystems where humans and intelligent agents co-create value neither could achieve alone.

Why "Agency" Matters

You might ask: why use the word *agency* at all? Why not call it the Age of AI, or Automation, or Intelligence?

Because words carry power. *Agency* captures something deeper—it's about ownership, intention, and the ability to act with purpose.

AI on its own is capability. Automation is execution. But agency is choice. It's the moment a system doesn't just do something—it *decides* why and how.

Think of it like this: an engine creates motion, but the driver creates direction. Now imagine AI that can co-drive—steering, accelerating, even rerouting when needed—while humans define vision and guardrails. That's what makes this era so profound. Agency implies responsibility, and now both humans and machines share that responsibility.

Humans + AI: The New Workforce

"We're at the beginning of a golden age of AI."
— Jeff Bezos

Let's make it real.

A **sales manager** once relied on gut instinct and quarterly reports. Today, an AI copilot surfaces trends in real time, crafts outreach, and recommends next steps. Her intuition expands into precision.

A **doctor** once struggled through fragmented charts. Now, AI summarizes patient histories, flags anomalies, and predicts complications. His agency extends into foresight.

A **startup founder** once juggled customers, operations, and growth. Today, agents handle onboarding, invoices, and FAQs. Her focus shifts from firefighting to vision.

This is the new workforce: humans and AI agents, complementing each other's strengths, scaling impact through partnership.

The Business Case

Why does this matter? Because shared agency is now the currency of competitiveness.

- **Speed.** Decision cycles that once took months now happen in minutes.
- **Scale.** Personalization and prediction at levels once impossible become daily realities.

- **Resilience.** Businesses that distribute intelligence adapt faster during crises.
- **Innovation.** Freed from repetitive work, humans have space for creativity and empathy.

Companies clinging to human-only models will slow down. Those who design human–AI ecosystems will move faster, serve smarter, and grow stronger.

Restoring Humanity to Work

"Technology is best when it brings people together."
— Matt Mullenweg

There's a fear that as AI takes on more, humans lose relevance. But when designed intentionally, the opposite is true.

Shared agency can give people back what bureaucracy and burnout have stolen—time, dignity, and creativity. For decades, workers were reduced to cogs: measured by hours, not outcomes. Now, intelligent systems can handle the drudgery, letting humans return to what only they can do—dream, design, connect, and lead.

This isn't about replacing people. It's about restoring humanity to work. But it only happens when leaders deploy AI to expand human potential, not diminish it. It takes policies that treat agency as a right, not a privilege—and individuals willing to reinvent, not retreat.

The Risks of Misalignment

Of course, shared agency comes with shared risk.

- If AI acts without values, outcomes drift from ethics.
- If humans abdicate too much control, critical thinking erodes.
- If only a few hold the keys, inequality deepens.

This transformation isn't automatically utopian. It's a fork in the road. We must choose whether agency will elevate humanity—or erode it.

That's why this book exists: to map the path forward.

A Compass for the Intelligent Era

Here's the compass I've lived by, and the one that shapes the playbooks ahead:

- **Vision over Tools.** Don't chase features. Start with the future you want to create.
- **Collaboration over Control.** Build ecosystems, not hierarchies. Treat AI as partner, not servant.
- **Values over Velocity.** Move fast—but stay anchored in purpose.
- **Resilience over Perfection.** Don't design for certainty. Design to adapt.

This compass won't eliminate risk—but it ensures we move with intention, not reaction.

From Survival to Thrival

"The purpose of business is to create and keep a customer."
— Peter Drucker

Many organizations are stuck in survival mode—battling shortages, uncertainty, and burnout. But survival isn't the goal. Thrival is.

This era isn't about scraping through disruption; it's about using it as fuel. Designing companies where resilience is built-in, customers feel understood before they ask, and employees feel empowered instead of drained.

That's what shared agency makes possible: not just surviving storms, but rising stronger because of them.

The Phoenix Lesson

Every era of transformation demands a rebirth. Like the phoenix, we must let the old burn to make space for the new. This moment is that fire. Yes, it's disruptive—but it's also liberating. It's our chance to rebuild work itself: to merge intelligence and empathy, precision and creativity, scale and soul.

A Call to Builders and Leaders

This is not a conclusion—it's an invitation.

If you're a **leader**, don't just implement AI—design for empowerment.

If you're a **builder**, don't just automate—humanize.

If you're an **individual**, don't fear what's coming—partner with it. Expand your impact by learning how to think *with* machines.

Because this shift is already here. The only question left is: will you shape it, or be shaped by it?

THE EVOLUTION OF AGENCY

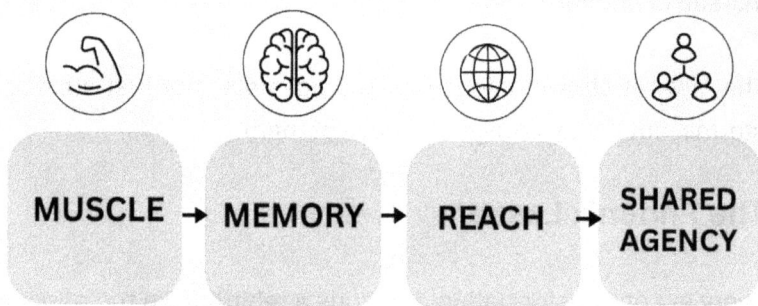

MUSCLE → **MEMORY** → **REACH** → **SHARED AGENCY**

When historians look back, they won't call this the age of automation—they'll call it the moment humans learned to think, act, and create with intelligence that could learn back.

If agency is the new foundation, intelligence is the force that fuels it.

In the next chapter, we'll explore what that means: how we move from linear automation to adaptive, reasoning systems—and why *intelligence*, not just automation, will define the next decade of growth.

CHAPTER 2

From Automation to Intelligence

How the World Is Shifting from Linear Execution to Living Intelligence

"AI is the new electricity."
— Andrew Ng

Every revolution starts quietly. Machines replaced muscle. Software replaced paperwork. But what's happening now—the rise from automation to intelligence—isn't just another productivity upgrade. It's a consciousness shift inside business itself.

Automation helped us *do more*. Intelligence helps us *become more*.

It's the difference between a machine that obeys commands and a system that *learns, reasons, and acts with purpose*. Between a workflow that follows rules—and an intelligent network that rewrites them to deliver better outcomes.

Welcome to the age where systems don't just execute; they evolve.

The End of Linear Automation

Automation was humanity's first attempt at scale. We scripted tasks, codified rules, and taught machines to repeat what worked. It made us faster, cheaper, more predictable.

But linear automation—robotic process automation (RPA), macros, pre-set triggers—was designed for a stable world. When inputs changed, it broke.

Automation was like a train: powerful but stuck on rails. One detour, one unexpected signal, and the whole system stopped.

And for years, that was enough. Efficiency was the dream. But efficiency alone doesn't build resilience.

The world moved faster than the systems we built to control it. And now, the very foundations of automation are cracking under the weight of complexity.

The Rise of Intelligence

Today, something entirely new is emerging. Machines are no longer just tools that *do what we say*—they're partners that *think with us*.

AI isn't a linear process. It's a living ecosystem of adaptive reasoning, self-learning, and autonomous action. It doesn't just execute workflows—it *designs better ones on the fly.*

We've crossed from the mechanical age to the cognitive age.

- **Adaptive** systems learn from real-time context, not static scripts.
- **Intelligent** systems make sense of ambiguity and nuance.
- **Agentic** systems take initiative toward goals, operating with human-like agency under ethical guardrails.

In this new world, intelligence isn't centralized. It's distributed— embedded in every product, customer touchpoint, and workflow.

Automation executed instructions.

Intelligence interprets intention.

And that single difference changes everything.

The Three Horizons of AI Evolution

1. **Automation — Doing Things Right** Repeatable, rule-based, cost-saving. Essential for consistency but fragile under change.
2. **Intelligence — Doing the Right Things** Adaptive systems that reason, optimize, and learn continuously. Efficiency meets context.
3. **Agentic AI — Deciding What to Do Next** Proactive AI that takes responsibility for outcomes within boundaries. Systems that *collaborate* with humans to drive growth, resilience, and creativity.

The future isn't about replacing human effort—it's about expanding human *agency.* Automation replaced muscle. Intelligence expands the mind.

From Static Systems to Living Networks

Think about your business. For years, you've probably optimized for processes: cleaner handoffs, automated triggers, defined SLAs. But even the best automation hits a wall when reality shifts.

Intelligent systems break that wall. They *flow.*

- They sense customer sentiment and adjust outreach instantly.
- They detect operational anomalies before they snowball.
- They re-prioritize tasks based on dynamic value, not fixed order.

This is what I call **Living Intelligence**—a system that learns, heals, and grows with you.

Imagine a network of digital agents across your organization, all collaborating toward a shared mission—anticipating needs, rerouting friction, and amplifying human judgment in real time. That's not automation. That's *SuperIntelligence in motion.*

Why Intelligence Wins

Linear automation optimized the past. Intelligent systems invent the future.

Here's why this shift is non-negotiable:

- **The World Is Nonlinear.** Static workflows can't survive dynamic markets.
- **Data Is Exploding.** Intelligence thrives where data overwhelms human capacity.
- **Customer Expectations Have Evolved.** They expect anticipation, not reaction.
- **Speed Is Everything.** Intelligent systems operate in milliseconds, not meetings.

In short, automation was built for stability. Intelligence thrives on change.

And if your business doesn't adapt, it won't just lag—it will *freeze*.

The Intelligence Playbook

This transformation is operational.

Here's how leaders begin the leap from automation to intelligence:

Step 1. Audit for Fragility

Find the processes that break when the environment shifts. These are your prime candidates for intelligent redesign.

Step 2. Redesign for Context

Layer adaptive intelligence into your workflows. Let systems learn from history, feedback, and environment—not just follow logic trees.

Step 3. Build Feedback Loops

Create living systems that evolve through continuous data ingestion. Intelligence grows through iteration.

Step 4. Empower Agentic Behavior

Start small. Allow AI to take action within boundaries. Let it schedule, recommend, and adjust autonomously—then expand scope as trust builds.

Step 5. Keep Humans in the Loop

Humans define meaning, ethics, and direction. AI executes and optimizes. It's not man *versus* machine—it's man *with* machine.

This isn't just an upgrade—it's a rewiring.

The New Value Equation

In the automation era, success was measured in cost savings. In the intelligence era, success is measured in *speed of adaptation*.

Automation asks: "How much can we save?"

Intelligence asks: "How fast can we evolve?"

This evolution shifts focus from execution to orchestration, from rigid processes to fluid ecosystems. And in that shift, new growth appears—because intelligent systems don't just reduce errors; they *discover opportunities*.

When systems begin to sense, learn, and act in unison, your organization stops *managing change* and starts *designing it*.

The Human Renaissance

Here's the irony: as AI grows smarter, humans grow more essential.

Automation once made us fear obsolescence. Intelligence brings us back to what makes us irreplaceable—judgment, empathy, creativity, and vision.

Agentic systems don't replace human agency; they *mirror it*. They remind us that intelligence without purpose is just noise.

The goal of SuperIntelligence isn't to outthink us—it's to *augment* us. To turn our ideas into living ecosystems of execution.

In the age of intelligence, humans are no longer task executors—they're system designers, storytellers, and orchestrators of meaning.

Closing: From Scripts to Symphonies

The Industrial Revolution gave us machines. The Digital Revolution gave us automation. The Intelligence Revolution gives us *agency*.

We're no longer writing instructions for systems to follow—we're designing systems that *think with us*.

And when intelligence becomes collaborative, not coded, business stops being mechanical and starts being alive.

This is not evolution by chance—it's transformation by design.

From automation to intelligence. From efficiency to emergence. From control to co-creation.

The **next chapter** of business isn't about doing things faster—it's about doing things *smarter, freer, and more human*.

Welcome to the rise of SuperIntelligence.

THREE HORIZONS OF AI EVOLUTION

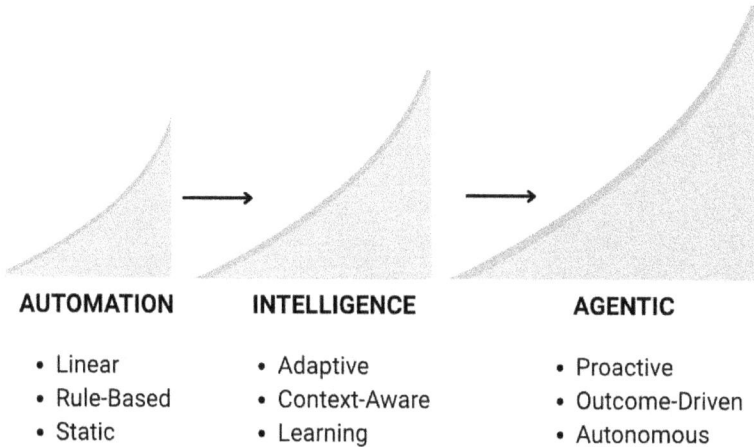

AUTOMATION	INTELLIGENCE	AGENTIC
• Linear	• Adaptive	• Proactive
• Rule-Based	• Context-Aware	• Outcome-Driven
• Static	• Learning	• Autonomous

AI Evolution Horizon

When intelligence meets customer experience, everything changes. The next chapter shows how AI reshapes not just operations—but the customer's very sense of agency.

CHAPTER 3

The Agentic Customer

How Hyper-Personalization and Predictive AI Redefine Customer Experience

From Passive Consumers to Agentic Customers

"Customer experience is the new battleground."

— Chris Pemberton

There was a time when "customer experience" meant a smile at checkout, a thank-you email, or a helpful support rep on the line. That era is gone. Today's customers are not passive participants in the value chain. They are *agentic*: active, informed, and in control. They expect companies to anticipate their needs, not just respond to them. They demand personalization that feels intimate, predictive, and seamless across every touchpoint.

We've crossed a threshold. The customer journey is no longer linear. It's a web of micro-moments, each influenced by context, history, and intent. And at the center of this transformation is **AI-driven**

hyper-personalization, technology that doesn't just reflect what customers say, but predicts what they *will* want, sometimes before they know it themselves.

The question for leaders is no longer *"How do we serve customers efficiently?"* but rather *"How do we empower agentic customers to co-create their experience, on their terms, at scale?"*

This is the agentic era, and hyper-personalization and predictive AI are its engine.

Defining the Agentic Customer

An **agentic customer** is one who:

- **Exerts control** over their journey, expecting brands to bend around their lifestyle, not the other way around.
- **Demands context-aware interactions** — they want brands to remember their history, preferences, and even mood in real time.
- **Values co-creation** — preferring products, services, and experiences that adapt dynamically to their feedback.
- **Rejects generic engagement** — they view "Dear Valued Customer" emails as insults.

Think about Netflix. When you log in, it doesn't hand you a static catalog. It curates your experience with uncanny accuracy, serving content based on your behavior, preferences, and the behaviors of people like you. Netflix is not just recommending; it's predicting. That's the essence of agentic engagement.

Contrast that with a traditional cable provider, where every customer gets the same package of 200 channels. That model feels prehistoric in comparison.

Agentic customers don't tolerate friction. They want the "Netflix effect" in healthcare, banking, retail, SaaS, and beyond. And if one company doesn't deliver, they switch to one that will.

The Rise of Hyper-Personalization

"We see our customers as invited guests to a party."
— Jeff Bezos

Personalization used to mean "Hi Rajitha" at the top of an email. **Hyper-personalization** means an entirely different level:

- *Real-time adaptation* of digital interfaces to your behavior.
- *Contextual offers* based on predictive analytics, not generic campaigns.
- *Dynamic journeys* that shift when your intent shifts.
- *Cross-channel intelligence* that follows you seamlessly from app to email to human support.

Here's an example:

> Imagine booking a hotel room. Traditional personalization gives you a "Welcome back, Rajitha!" email.

Hyper-personalization:

- Notice you've been searching for flights to Lisbon.
- Suggests a hotel with a family suite, since your past trips show you travel with kids.
- Offers a rose-garden view because your reviews consistently mention outdoor spaces.
- Pre-loads local recommendations aligned to your dining habits (vegan, spice-friendly, mid-range).
- Pushes an early check-in option because your flight lands at 6 a.m.

This isn't personalization. It's **preparation for your next move.** It's not static. It's predictive.

Hyper-personalization turns customers into partners in the experience. It signals: *"We see you. We know you. We've designed this for you."* That's agentic empowerment.

Predictive AI: Anticipating Needs Before They're Spoken

If hyper-personalization is the *what*, **predictive AI** is the *how*.

Predictive AI uses historical data, behavioral signals, and contextual inputs to forecast customer needs and trigger proactive actions. It's why Spotify serves you a playlist that feels like it read your mind, or how Amazon suggests products you didn't realize you wanted until you saw them.

Let's break this down with a framework I use:

The 3 Levels of Predictive Customer Experience

1. **Reactive** – Respond when the customer asks.
   - Example: Customer emails about a billing issue. Support fixes it.
   - Customer feels: "At least they handled it."
2. **Proactive** – Act before the customer asks.
   - Example: Airline notifies you of a gate change before you see the board.
   - Customer feels: "They're on top of things."
3. **Predictive Agentic** – Shape the journey based on what the customer *will* want.
   - Example: Banking app notices unusual spending, blocks fraud, and suggests a savings adjustment based on your goals.
   - Customer feels: "They're protecting my future, not just reacting."

Companies that master level 3 create not just loyalty but advocacy. Because when customers feel seen *and* anticipated, they trust.

Why This Matters: The Business Case

"People don't buy products;
they buy better versions of themselves."
— Unknown

Agentic customers aren't just a feel-good concept. They impact the bottom line. Consider:

- **Increased LTV (Lifetime Value):** McKinsey research shows personalization can drive a **10-15% revenue lift.** Hyper-personalization amplifies this further.
- **Reduced churn:** Predictive AI can flag "at-risk" customers early, enabling interventions before dissatisfaction turns into cancellation.
- **Faster growth loops:** Satisfied agentic customers share their experiences widely, becoming unpaid marketers.
- **Operational efficiency:** Anticipating needs reduces inbound support requests, slashing costs.

Put simply: companies that don't adopt agentic frameworks will bleed customers to those that do.

Case Studies: Agentic Experience in Action

1. **Healthcare – Cleveland Clinic**Using predictive AI, they anticipate patient needs by analyzing health records. For example, if a patient misses a refill, the system triggers outreach before a crisis occurs. Patients feel guided, not abandoned.
2. **Retail –** Nike's app doesn't just sell shoes. It tracks workouts, suggests gear, and personalizes experiences based on your activity data. Customers don't feel like buyers — they feel like athletes in partnership with Nike.
3. **B2B SaaS – Salesforce,** By embedding AI into customer success, Salesforce predicts account health scores, recommends upsell timing, and suggests interventions for

churn risks. This creates relationships where businesses feel their growth is actively supported.

Each example highlights a shift: companies no longer wait for customer input. They create **agentic ecosystems** that adapt dynamically to customer life.

The Trust Factor

Hyper-personalization and predictive AI can cross a fine line. What feels magical can quickly feel **creepy** if mishandled. Customers will abandon a brand that violates trust.

The antidote? **Transparency + Control.**

- **Transparency:** Be clear about how data is used. If an app recommends a product because of your browsing, say so.
- **Control:** Give customers the option to set boundaries. Let them dial up or down the level of personalization.

Agentic customers want empowerment, not surveillance. The best brands give them the steering wheel.

Designing for the Agentic Era: A Playbook

"The customer is the hero of our story."

— Ann Handley

So how do you, as a leader, build agentic experiences? Here's a framework I use with clients:

Step 1. Know the Customer as a Whole Human

Move beyond demographics. Map context: goals, moods, history, micro-moments. Use AI to unify data across channels into a single narrative.

Step 2. Anticipate with Responsibility

Build predictive models that suggest, not dictate. Let customers choose from intelligent options.

Step 3. Design Adaptive Journeys

No more rigid funnels. Build systems that adapt in real time — if a customer pauses at step 3, the journey shifts automatically.

Step 4. Balance Automation and Humanity

Agentic customers don't want bots alone. They want seamless handoffs between AI and human support when stakes are high.

Step 5. Measure What Matters

Go beyond NPS. Track **Agentic Empowerment Metrics**:

- % of interactions resolved before customer effort.
- % of predictive interventions accepted by customers.
- Time saved per customer through automation.

The Agentic Flywheel

Let's visualize this as a flywheel:

1. **Collect Data** →
2. **Predict Behavior** →
3. **Personalize Experience** →
4. **Customer Feels Empowered** →
5. **Shares Feedback & Data** →
6. **Improved Prediction**

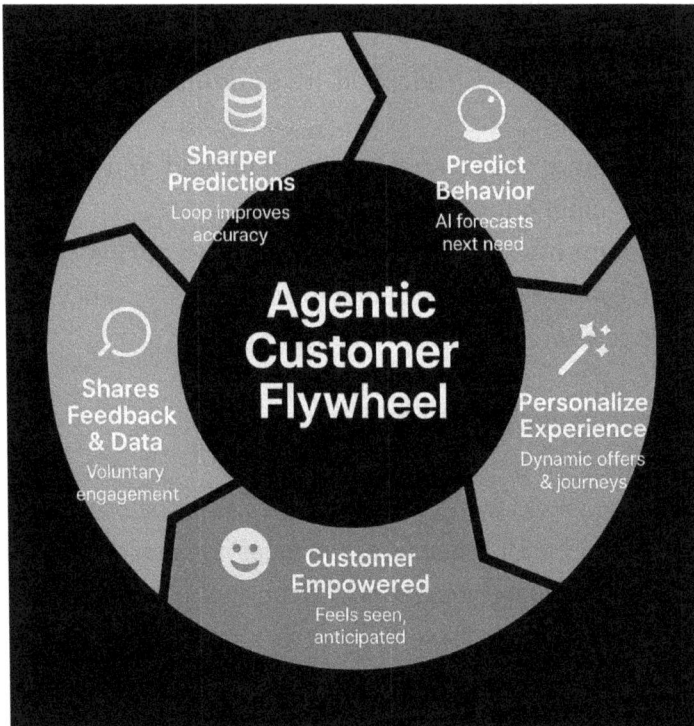

Agentic Customer FlyWheel

The more customers feel empowered, the more data they willingly share. This creates a virtuous loop where personalization deepens, predictions sharpen, and loyalty compounds.

Leadership in the Agentic Age

As executives, we have to ask: *Are we building systems for yesterday's customer or tomorrow's?*

The agentic customer is not a trend. It's the new baseline. Companies that resist will wither. Companies that embrace will redefine categories.

This isn't just about tech adoption. It's a **cultural transformation.**

- Leaders must shift from command-and-control to co-creation.
- Teams must embrace data as narrative, not just numbers.
- Organizations must center the customer's agency in every decision.

A Personal Note

I think back to moments in my own journey as a Customer Success leader. One of the most painful experiences is watching a customer churn — not because your product wasn't good, but because you failed to anticipate their evolving needs.

I've sat in executive meetings where we celebrated renewals while quietly ignoring the silent signals of disengagement. I've also seen the opposite: teams that leaned into predictive insights, reached out before the customer even realized they had an issue, and turned near-churn accounts into raving advocates.

The difference wasn't more budget, more people, or more slides. It was a mindset shift: from **reacting** to **empowering.**

Looking Ahead: The Next Horizon

Agentic customers are only the beginning. The next frontier is **agentic ecosystems** where customers, companies, and AI systems interact fluidly.

Picture this:

- Your home energy system predicts a heatwave and auto-adjusts usage to save costs — while suggesting a solar upgrade.
- Your HR platform predicts employee burnout signals and offers wellness options before attrition spikes.
- Your SaaS tool dynamically evolves features based on aggregated customer intent, without waiting for roadmap votes.

This isn't science fiction. It's arriving faster than most realize.

Call to Action

If you're reading this as a leader, here's the challenge:

1. **Audit your customer experience today.** Where are you still reactive? Where could predictive insights change the game?
2. **Pilot one hyper-personalized journey.** Start small. Test. Iterate. Scale.
3. **Build trust as a design principle.** Without it, personalization collapses.
4. **Shift your culture.** Teach teams to view customers not as endpoints, but as *co-creators of value.*

Because the future of customer experience isn't about serving more efficiently. It's about empowering customers to become *agentic partners* in the journey.

Final Thought

The companies that thrive in the next decade will be those that understand this truth:

Customers don't just want to be served. They want to be seen, anticipated, and empowered.

That's the promise of hyper-personalization and predictive AI.

That's the power of the agentic customer.

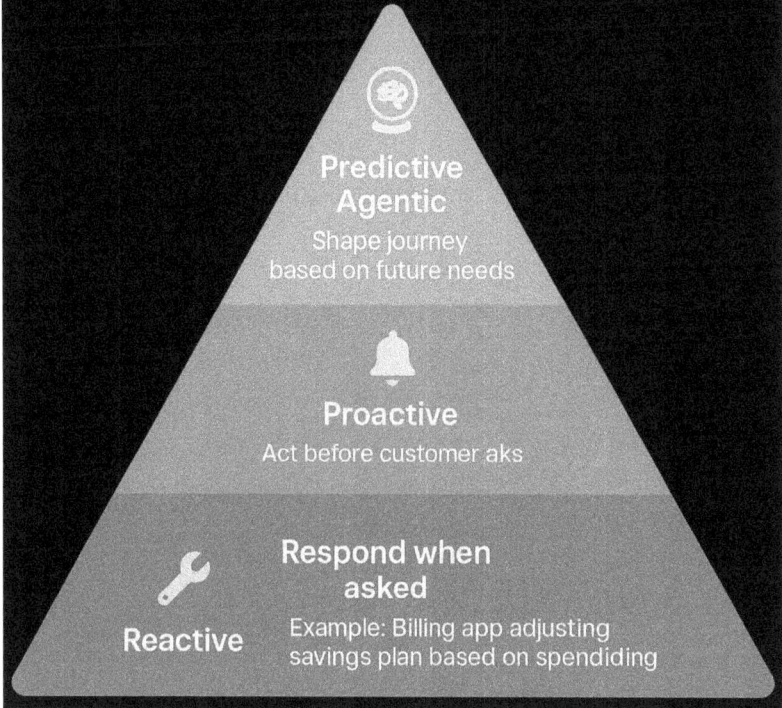

3 Levels of Predictive CX

Predictive Agentic
Shape journey based on future needs

Proactive
Act before customer aks

Reactive — **Respond when asked**
Example: Billing app adjusting savings plan based on spendiding

Nowhere is trust more critical than in money. Let's see how FinTech is redefining trust, risk, and growth through Agentic AI.

CHAPTER 4

FinTech's AI Inflection Point

Transforming Trust, Risk, and Financial Growth with Agentic AI

The Moment of Inflection

Every industry hits a "no-turning-back" moment.

For retail, it was e-commerce.

For media, it was streaming.

For finance, it is **Agentic AI**—a point where trust, risk, and growth are rewritten in real time.

Financial services have always courted technology. Banks built mainframes before most offices had night-time electricity. Algorithmic trading, fraud detection, and digital wallets all moved the industry forward. But the rise of *agentic, hyper-personalized AI* isn't another wave—it's a **tectonic shift**.

Finance isn't only about money. It's about **trust**—the invisible contract that a loan, investment, or paycheck will hold its promise. And AI isn't merely automating tasks; it's **reshaping belief systems**.

We now enter an era where predictive intelligence *anticipates* risk before it appears, where digital advisors *co-create* financial paths, and where fraud systems *outthink* bad actors.

Handled well, this inflection won't just change how money moves—it will redefine what we trust, how we grow, and who participates in financial progress.

Trust as the Currency of FinTech

Money has always mirrored confidence. A dollar's worth depends on collective belief; markets exist because millions agree on tomorrow's potential. Yet that belief is fragile. The 2008 collapse and scandals like FTX proved how fast digital faith can evaporate.

Enter Agentic AI.

Unlike static models, agentic systems are dynamic, self-optimizing, and context-aware. They learn and personalize in real time. Picture a *digital trust advisor* inside your banking app—aware of your goals and risk tolerance, cross-checking global fraud signals, regulation changes, and market shifts.

Trust moves from a **fragile human construct** to a **continuously reinforced digital fabric**.

Key shifts:

- **Hyper-personalized credibility** beyond credit scores— using behavioral patterns, payment rhythms, even communication tone.
- **Transparent auditability**—explainable AI that restores fairness and accountability.
- **Proactive fraud defense**—predicting and blocking threats before loss occurs.

When trust becomes programmable, *financial inclusion accelerates*. Those once labeled "too risky" gain new access. It's not only an economic leap—it's a social one.

Risk: From Reactive to Predictive

If trust is finance's foundation, risk is its constant shadow. Traditional risk management reacts—add buffers, hedge bets, enforce controls. Agentic AI makes it **predictive and adaptive**.

Yesterday: manual compliance teams drowning in paperwork.

Today: AI detects anomalies *after* they occur.

Tomorrow: **AI risk sentinels** simulate millions of "what-if" scenarios continuously.

A mid-size bank could monitor not just balance sheets but sentiment, geopolitics, even climate data to foresee loan defaults. A flood triggers automatic recalibration; a viral "bank-run" post prompts pre-emptive liquidity moves. Cyber attacks not only fail—the system self-heals its perimeter.

Risk evolves from *event* to *ecosystem*.

Growth: From Transactional to Transformational

Historically, growth meant more transactions—accounts, loans, payments. But **volume isn't valuable.** Agentic AI enables growth that's *transformational.*

- **Individuals:** AI advisors rebalance savings, taxes, and investments dynamically—anticipating life shifts and empowering smarter habits.
- **SMBs:** POS systems forecast downturns, renegotiate suppliers, and recommend micro-loans to smooth cash flow.
- **Institutions:** AI agents coordinate compliance, engagement, and trading—building resilience instead of fragile scale.

The new question isn't *"How much did we process?"* but *"How intelligently did we grow?"*

The Ethical Imperative

With every revolution comes risk. When trust is programmable, **who writes the code?** When risk is predictive, **who defines acceptable loss?**

Bias lives in data. If yesterday's lending excluded minority-owned businesses, uncorrected AI will replicate that harm—faster and at scale. If fraud models learn from narrow samples, entire populations remain unprotected.

Thus, FinTech's inflection isn't only *what* we build—it's *how* *responsibly* we build it.

Guiding principles:

- **Transparency** → Explain decisions clearly to regulators and customers.
- **Fairness** → Test for bias, close equity gaps.
- **Accountability** → Humans remain responsible; AI augments, not absolves.
- **Security** → Treat data as entrusted capital, not fuel.

Future finance will be judged not by speed but by **integrity of implementation**.

Where It's Already Happening

1. **Agentic Wealth Management** — Robo-advisors evolve into adaptive partners that adjust portfolios in sync with life events.
2. **Next-Gen Fraud Defense** — Payment processors simulate attacks to anticipate fraud strategies, cutting false positives and losses.
3. **Credit Inclusion via Behavioral AI** — Micro-lenders use utility and mobile data to grant fair credit beyond FICO biases.

4. **Compliance as Code** — Startups embed regulations into real-time AI agents, reducing manual audits and costs.

These aren't prototypes. They signal that the inflection is *now*.

The Human in the Loop

If AI is so smart, where do humans fit? Everywhere trust requires empathy.

Money is emotional. Investments tie to hope; insurance reflects fear. AI crunches numbers, but humans carry meaning. Agentic AI *elevates* financial professionals—it removes drudgery so they can listen, guide, and reassure.

The winning FinTechs won't remove people—they'll **redefine their purpose** around relationship and trust.

The Road Ahead

Handled with care, this inflection will democratize wealth and make trust renewable instead of scarce. Mishandled, it could automate bias and erode faith entirely.

The question isn't *if* Agentic AI will transform finance—it already has. The question is whether leaders and regulators will rise to its responsibility.

Finance's future isn't a tech story. It's a **trust story, a risk story, a growth story.** Those who understand that will build better companies and stronger economies.

Closing Thought

FinTech's AI inflection point isn't about faster apps. It's about **re-architecting belief** in the systems that hold our economy together.

Trust becomes programmable. Risk becomes predictive. Growth becomes transformational.

For the first time, finance has the tools to serve not just the wealthy but everyone ready to believe again.

That is the promise of Agentic AI in FinTech.

▨ Recipe Card | FinTech's AI Inflection Point

Transform Trust, Risk & Growth with Agentic AI

Core Ingredients

- **Agentic AI Frameworks** – self-optimizing, context-aware systems
- **Trust Signals** – behavioral + contextual data beyond credit scores
- **Risk Simulation Engines** – predictive "what-if" models
- **Compliance Protocols** – ethics + fairness baked into code
- **Human Expertise** – empathy and judgment for high-stakes moments

Preparation | How to Build

1. **Recode Trust** → replace generic credit scores with personalized credibility maps; ensure explainability.
2. **Shift Risk Management** → move from alerts to continuous simulation; factor macro signals.
3. **Design for Growth** → build transformational partnerships that coach and include.
4. **Build Ethical Guardrails** → transparency, fairness, accountability in every model.
5. **Keep Humans in the Loop** → AI predicts; humans build trust.

Quick Wins

1. Launch AI-driven fraud shields to cut false positives.
2. Pilot AI-powered micro-lending for underserved communities.
3. Automate compliance through embedded regulatory agents.

Serving Suggestions (Who Benefits)

1. **Banks & Credit Unions:** higher trust, lower loss.
2. **SMBs & Startups:** predictive cash-flow visibility.
3. **Investors:** adaptive wealth strategies.
4. **Consumers:** clarity and confidence.

Signature Insight

FinTech's inflection point isn't speed—it's **trust by design**. The leaders who balance AI's intelligence with human empathy will own the future of finance.

If AI can rebuild trust in finance, imagine what it can do for life itself. Healthcare is next—and lives literally depend on getting it right.

CHAPTER 5

Healthcare Without Friction

The role of AI agents in improving care delivery, patient experience, and operational efficiency

The Waiting Room Test

If you want to understand the state of healthcare today, just sit in a waiting room.

Clipboards with paper forms. A receptionist asking for the same insurance card you gave them three times already. The buzz of patients trying to figure out if they'll be called before their parking meter runs out.

This is the reality: healthcare is still drowning in friction. Friction between patients and providers. Friction between data systems. Friction between insurers and hospitals. Friction that delays treatment, frustrates families, and costs billions in wasted resources.

Now imagine this: instead of friction, the system flows. The moment you walk in, your information is already synced across providers. Your AI agent checked you in last night, verified your insurance, and even adjusted your appointment time because it noticed traffic patterns in your city. Your physician spends time talking to you—not toggling between five screens. And when you leave, your personalized care plan is in your inbox, explained in plain English with reminders that adjust based on your behavior.

That's healthcare without friction. And that's where AI agents change the game.

Why Healthcare Needs Agents, Not Just Algorithms

Healthcare has already seen waves of technology: electronic health records, telemedicine, even predictive analytics. But let's be honest—they often added complexity instead of removing it. Doctors became data clerks. Patients became password managers.

AI agents are different. They're not just algorithms spitting out probabilities; they're **autonomous collaborators**. Agents can **act**, not just analyze. They don't wait for you to log in and pull a report; they anticipate, coordinate, and execute.

Think of them as the invisible staff member who never gets tired:

- They chase down prior authorizations at 2 AM.
- They reconcile conflicting prescriptions before they reach the pharmacy.

- They proactively nudge patients who are about to miss their follow-up.

This is more than automation—it's orchestration.

The 3 Fronts of Transformation

AI agents in healthcare will drive transformation on three critical fronts:

1. Care Delivery – From Reactive to Predictive

Today, care is still mostly reactive. You get sick → you see a doctor → you get treatment. AI agents flip the model. They monitor signals, detect risk early, and shape care before problems escalate.

- A diabetic patient's glucose sensor doesn't just ping; their AI agent alerts both the patient and provider, schedules a telehealth check-in, and adjusts reminders for diet and activity.
- In hospitals, AI agents triage incoming patients by analyzing vitals, symptoms, and history in real-time, helping ER staff prioritize without guesswork.

This isn't replacing doctors. It's making them superhuman.

2. Patient Experience – From Confusing to Clear

If there's one universal truth: patients are overwhelmed. Bills that look like tax codes. Medical jargon that feels like another language. Endless waiting.

AI agents become interpreters, guides, and advocates.

- They explain treatment plans in plain language, tailored to your level of health literacy.
- They book appointments, handle reminders, and even reorder prescriptions automatically.
- They act as the single point of contact—so patients stop bouncing between call centers, websites, and portals.

Healthcare becomes something patients can **navigate, not survive**.

3. Operational Efficiency – From Waste to Flow

Healthcare burns cash in administrative overhead. Studies show up to **25% of U.S. healthcare spending is waste,** much of it tied to inefficiency, paperwork, and coordination gaps.

AI agents are the ultimate friction removers:

- Automating claims submission and insurance pre-approvals.
- Reconciling records across fragmented systems.
- Forecasting staff schedules and resource demand.

Hospitals run smoother. Staff burnout decreases. Costs come down.

The Trust Equation

But here's the catch: healthcare is about trust. You can't just throw AI at the problem and expect acceptance. Patients and providers must feel that these agents are safe, ethical, and transparent.

The trust equation has three parts:

1. **Accuracy** – If an AI agent is wrong, it's not a typo—it can be life or death. Models must be trained on validated, diverse, and bias-aware data.
2. **Transparency** – Patients need to know *why* the AI recommended a step, not just what it recommended. Explainability isn't optional.
3. **Human Oversight** – AI agents don't replace doctors; they extend them. The human remains in the loop for decisions that require judgment, empathy, and nuance.

Trust isn't a side feature—it's the foundation. Without it, adoption collapses.

Stories from the Field

Let's look at some real-world sparks of this transformation:

- **Cleveland Clinic** piloted an AI scheduling agent that reduced no-shows by 19% by automatically rescheduling and sending behavior-based reminders.
- **Mayo Clinic** deployed an AI agent for radiology that scans images and flags anomalies for review—cutting time-to-diagnosis by up to 30%.

- **Telehealth startups** now use AI-driven intake agents that capture symptoms conversationally, pre-fill physician notes, and cut visit prep time in half.

These are not experiments in a lab—they're real use cases already reducing friction. The next leap is weaving them together across the entire care journey.

The Healthcare Without Friction Playbook

To bring this vision to life, organizations can't just "buy AI." They need a **playbook** for deploying AI agents that create flow instead of adding noise.

Step 1: Map the Friction Points

- Identify where patients, providers, and staff experience the most pain (billing, scheduling, data silos, prior authorizations).
- Quantify the impact (e.g., missed revenue, staff hours lost, patient complaints).

Step 2: Deploy Agent Pilots Where Friction is Highest

- Start with high-impact, low-risk use cases: appointment scheduling, patient reminders, insurance verification.
- Use agents that can **act**, not just analyze.

Step 3: Build Patient-Centric Design

- Ensure AI agents communicate in natural, empathetic language.
- Create interfaces where patients can choose human escalation anytime.

Step 4: Integrate with Workflows, Not Over Them

- Plug AI agents into existing EHRs, CRMs, and billing systems.
- Avoid forcing staff to learn "yet another tool."

Step 5: Monitor, Learn, Adapt

- Set metrics: reduced no-shows, faster claims, shorter wait times, higher patient satisfaction.
- Continuously tune models with clinician oversight and patient feedback loops.

Step 6: Scale Beyond Admin

- Once trust is built, expand to predictive care models, chronic disease management, and personalized wellness plans.
- Shift from "admin assistant" to "care partner."

Step 7: Anchor in Trust and Compliance

- Bake in explainability, data privacy, and ethical safeguards.
- Ensure every action has a clear audit trail.

This playbook isn't about replacing people—it's about **restoring humanity** to healthcare by stripping away the clutter.

The Human Dividend

What happens when we actually achieve healthcare without friction?

- **Doctors spend more time with patients, not paperwork.**
- **Patients feel cared for, not processed.**
- **Costs shrink, access expands, and outcomes improve.**

But beyond the metrics, there's a deeper dividend: dignity.

Healthcare, at its core, is about human connection. Right now, friction suffocates that connection. AI agents—when designed responsibly—can clear the space for empathy to breathe again.

Imagine your physician actually making eye contact because the AI agent already filled the chart. Imagine your elderly parent getting a check-in from an AI care companion that notices subtle changes in speech or movement and alerts a nurse before a fall happens. Imagine a system that feels seamless, personalized, and humane.

That's not science fiction. That's what we build when we stop asking AI to just process data and start letting it **shape experience.**

Closing Thought: From Transaction to Transformation

Every industry has its friction points, but healthcare's are uniquely consequential. The stakes are measured in lives.

AI agents aren't a magic cure, but they're the closest thing we've seen to a systemic relief valve. They hold the power to transform healthcare from a labyrinth of transactions into a flow of care experiences.

This chapter isn't a prediction—it's a blueprint. The tools exist. The urgency is undeniable. The only question is: do we have the courage to move beyond incremental fixes and design a healthcare system that finally flows?

Because when we do, the waiting room test disappears. Patients walk in, get cared for, and walk out with clarity—not confusion. That's healthcare without friction.

"What if small businesses could harness the same intelligence hospitals and banks use? They can—and they already are."

CHAPTER 6

SMBs as Giants

Why SMBs Can Now Scale Like Enterprises with Digital-First AI Strategies

The Underdog Advantage

"Do what you do so well that they will want to see it again."

— Walt Disney

For decades, small and mid-sized businesses (SMBs) have been seen as the underdogs of the marketplace—scrappy, resourceful, hustling just to keep up with the giants. They couldn't match the budgets, global reach, or armies of specialists that enterprises relied on. At best, SMBs carved out niches, grew slowly, and often plateaued when complexity outpaced their resources.

But here's the shift: in the digital-first era powered by AI, the underdog isn't at a disadvantage anymore. In fact, SMBs now have a once-in-a-generation opportunity to leapfrog larger competitors.

Think about it—enterprises are like cargo ships. They're massive, resource-heavy, and hard to steer. SMBs, on the other hand, are speedboats. With AI tools now available on demand—often at subscription prices of a few hundred dollars a month—SMBs can harness the same (or even more advanced) capabilities that once required multimillion-dollar IT investments.

SMBs can now scale like enterprises—without becoming bloated enterprises themselves.

The Digital-First AI Revolution

AI has removed the friction points that used to crush SMB growth. Let's unpack a few examples:

1. **Automation of Manual Workflows** Tasks that once ate up countless hours like, bookkeeping, scheduling, invoicing, customer follow-ups, are now automated end-to-end. SMBs can redeploy human time into strategy, innovation, and customer care rather than paperwork.
2. **Predictive Insights** AI doesn't just crunch numbers—it interprets them. SMBs can now forecast sales trends, predict inventory needs, and even spot churn risks the way only Fortune 500 companies could afford to do a decade ago.
3. **AI-Powered Customer Experience** Chatbots, hyper-personalized recommendations, and automated service flows are available out of the box. Your corner retail store can deliver the same kind of personalization as Amazon without writing a line of code.

4. **Affordable Cloud Infrastructure** Enterprise-grade CRM, ERP, and data platforms are offered as SaaS. You no longer need a data center to compete—just a Wi-Fi connection and a credit card.

The critical difference? SMBs can implement these tools faster, with less bureaucracy, and adapt as markets shift.

Case Study Snapshot: From Local Shop to Global Reach

Take the example of a boutique skincare brand in North Carolina. Just five years ago, their growth was limited to local farmers' markets and word-of-mouth. Then they adopted a digital-first AI strategy:

- **AI-driven e-commerce** gave them global storefronts overnight.
- **Predictive marketing** targeted new customers based on purchasing behavior across the U.S. and Europe.
- **Automated fulfillment tools** optimized shipping routes, reducing costs by 18%.

Within 24 months, they weren't just a local shop anymore—they are exporting to six countries, with a lean team of under 20 employees. That's SMBs scaling like giants.

Why SMBs Are Better Positioned Than Enterprises

Enterprises will always have resources, but in this new age, **resources don't equal advantage but speed and adaptability do**. Here's why SMBs have the edge:

1. **Less Bureaucracy = Faster Decisions** Enterprises can take months (sometimes years) to adopt a new tool. SMBs can test and implement within days. In the AI era, speed beats size.
2. **Cost Efficiency at Scale** AI levels the playing field. What once cost millions in data scientists and infrastructure can now be accessed through APIs and platforms like OpenAI, Co-Pilot, HubSpot, ChurnZero or Zendesk for a fraction of the cost.
3. **Customer Obsession by Design** SMBs are closer to their customers. With AI, they can scale that intimacy instead of losing it. Think hyper-local personalization amplified globally.
4. **Experimentation Culture** Enterprises worry about risk, governance, and compliance. SMBs experiment, pivot, and learn. AI thrives in environments where iteration is fast and fearless.

The Digital-First AI Playbook for SMBs

To turn potential into scale, SMBs need a **playbook**. Think of this as the recipe card for scaling like a giant.

Step 1: Audit Your Workflows

Ask: Where are my team and I spending time on repetitive, low-value tasks?

- Automate bookkeeping (QuickBooks + AI assistants).
- Automate customer scheduling (Calendly + AI reminders).
- Automate HR workflows (BambooHR with AI-enabled recruitment).

Outcome: Free up at least 20–30% of your team's time for higher-value work.

Step 2: Build Your Digital-First Stack

Ask: Do I have a tech backbone designed for AI-first, not just digitization?

- **CRM:** HubSpot or Zoho with AI-powered insights.
- **Marketing Automation:** Jasper or Copy.ai for campaigns.
- **Operations:** Airtable or Notion with AI integrations.
- **Customer Success:** Digital-first platforms like Gainsight PX or Intercom AI.

Outcome: A lightweight, scalable digital ecosystem with enterprise-grade power.

Step 3: Unlock Predictive Intelligence

Ask: Can I see what's coming before it happens?

- Predict churn by analyzing customer behavior.
- Forecast revenue using AI-driven sales analytics.
- Model inventory and supply chain needs with predictive algorithms.

Outcome: Fewer surprises, more confidence in growth planning.

Step 4: Hyper-Personalize Customer Experience

Ask: Am I delivering "giant-level" experiences with SMB warmth?

- Deploy AI chat bots for 24/7 engagement.
- Personalize e-commerce recommendations.
- Use generative AI to craft proposals tailored to each customer.

Outcome: Customers feel seen and valued—at scale.

Step 5: Go Global, Digitally

Ask: What's stopping me from selling beyond my ZIP code?

- AI-driven translation tools break language barriers.
- Cross-border payment systems simplify transactions.
- Logistics AI optimizes global shipping routes.

Outcome: A global footprint without global overhead.

From Survival Mode to Scale Mode

Many SMBs operate in survival mode: chasing invoices, juggling staff, reacting to problems. AI flips this script. When workflows are automated, insights are predictive, and customer engagement is digitized, leaders can finally focus on **scale mode**—strategic growth, new markets, and innovation.

It's not about replacing people with machines. It's about freeing people to work on what matters most.

Mindset Shift: From SMB to "Giant in the Making"

Scaling like a giant isn't just about tech—it's about mindset. SMB leaders need to reframe how they see themselves.

- **From Limited to Unlimited**: Your reach is no longer capped by geography or headcount.
- **From Reactive to Predictive**: AI allows you to anticipate, not just respond.
- **From Cost-Focused to Value-Creating**: Instead of asking, "What can we afford?" ask, "What value can we unlock?"

This mindset shift is what separates the SMBs who stay small from those who rise as giants in their category.

Playbook in Action: SMB Scaling Scenarios

Let's run through some **scenarios** of how SMBs can deploy digital-first AI strategies.

1. The Local Restaurant

- AI chatbots handle reservations and customer inquiries.
- Predictive ordering systems reduce food waste.
- Personalized offers sent to regulars boost loyalty.

Impact: Increased revenue + reduced costs = enterprise-level margins.

2. The Construction Firm

- AI project management tools track labor and supply chains.
- Drones and AI-powered imaging ensure safety compliance.
- Predictive bidding models improve win rates.

Impact: Competing head-to-head with national firms.

3. The Freelance Agency

- AI handles client onboarding, invoicing, and follow-ups.
- AI-powered creative tools speed up content delivery.
- Predictive analytics identify the most profitable client segments.

Impact: One-person agencies scale to serve dozens of global clients.

Here are some interesting Metrics

- **47% of SMBs** that implemented AI tools in 2023 reported revenue growth within the first year.
- **63% of SMB leaders** said automation reduced operational costs by at least 15%.
- **2 out of 3 SMBs** using predictive AI said they outperformed larger competitors in customer satisfaction scores.

This is not some AI hype, but it is AI happening.

Challenges to Watch Out For

Of course, scaling like a giant doesn't mean there are no risks. SMBs must navigate:

- **Over Reliance on Tools**: Tech is only as good as the strategy behind it.
- **Data Privacy & Compliance**: Even SMBs need to take security seriously.
- **Change Management**: Staff may resist AI adoption if not trained and motivated.

The key is to adopt with intention, not blindly.

The Future Belongs to SMB Giants

We're entering an age where **scale is no longer defined by size—it's defined by intelligence.** SMBs that embrace AI as their co-pilot will operate with the muscle of enterprises but the agility of startups.

The beauty? You don't need to "become corporate" to scale. You can keep your culture, your close customer ties, and your speed—while unlocking exponential growth.

The giants of tomorrow won't necessarily be born as Fortune 500s. They'll be SMBs who dared to think like giants, act digitally first, and put AI at the center of their strategy.

Bonus Blue Print: The Agentic Tech Stack for Entrepreneurs & SMB Leaders

In the new era of intelligent business, your tech stack isn't just a set of tools—it's your strategic co-founder. AI is the great equalizer, allowing small and mid-sized businesses to scale like enterprises without losing agility. This section outlines how to design an Agentic Tech Stack that automates, learns, and grows with you—so your company can operate with enterprise intelligence and startup speed.

The Agentic Framework: Build → Automate → Scale

Build Establish your foundation—systems, workflows, and clarity around your customer and data.

Automate Remove manual friction. Free up 30–40% of your team's time by letting AI handle repetitive tasks.

Scale Layer intelligence into operations, marketing, and customer experience to create exponential growth.

The Implementation Roadmap

1. **Phase 1 – Core Infrastructure:** Set up Notion, CRM, and automation backbone.
2. **Phase 2 – AI Enablement:** Add Precision dashboard + meeting AI (Granola.ai).
3. **Phase 3 – Customer & Growth AI:** Deploy AI sales caller, marketing AI, and CX automation.
4. **Phase 4 – Scale Mode:** Build your company brain (BuddyPro.ai or custom GPT).

Founder Insight: From Chaos to Clarity

A boutique e-commerce brand used this exact playbook—automating 70% of admin tasks and cutting operational costs by 25%. Within 90 days, they tripled their customer reach with an AI-powered CX layer. This demonstrates the power of designing an intelligent business, not just running one.

Call to Action

If you're ready to design your own Agentic Tech Stack, you don't have to do it alone.

Book a 1-hour Strategy Session with me to map your systems, identify automation opportunities, and build your AI-powered foundation. This is how you stop reacting to disruption—and start orchestrating it. Contact me via email: contact@rajitharupani.com

In the next era of business, founders won't scale through more people—they'll scale through more intelligence. Your tech stack isn't just infrastructure—it's your new growth engine. Build it right, and AI doesn't replace you—it amplifies you.

"Technology can scale a company, but only teams make it thrive. Let's design teams where humans and AI collaborate seamlessly."

CHECKPOINT: BECOMING AGENTIC

The next evolution isn't what we build, but *how we build together* — teams that blend human creativity and AI precision.

CHAPTER 7

Building Agentic Teams

Designing Organizations Where Humans and AI Collaborate Seamlessly

The Shift From Tools to Teammates

"Great things in business are never done by one person."

— Steve Jobs

For decades, we've thought of technology as a tool—a hammer, a spreadsheet, an app. Something you use, and then put down. But in the age of Agentic AI, technology isn't just a tool anymore. It's a teammate.

This is a fundamental mindset shift.

Tools execute instructions. Teammates co-create outcomes. Tools are reactive. Teammates are proactive, predictive, and adaptive.

And when you start to see AI agents not as apps on your desktop, but as colleagues on your team, it changes everything about how you design organizations, hire talent, measure success, and build culture.

That's what this chapter is about: how to build **Agentic Teams**— organizations where humans and AI collaborate seamlessly, amplifying strengths and filling one another's gaps.

Why Agentic Teams Matter Now

The speed of business today doesn't leave room for inefficiency. Customers expect real-time responses, personalization at scale, and frictionless experiences. Employees want meaningful work, not endless repetitive tasks. Leaders need sharper visibility, not lagging dashboards.

Traditional team structures—silos, hierarchies, static roles—simply weren't built for this reality.

Agentic Teams, on the other hand, are:

- **Adaptive by design.** AI agents learn, predict, and evolve with the business.
- **Human-first.** People get to focus on creativity, empathy, and strategic judgment.
- **Always-on.** Agents don't sleep, get sick, or take vacations.
- **Boundary-less.** Teams can scale across time zones, languages, and functions instantly.

This is not a "future state." It's already happening. Healthcare is using AI agents as care coordinators. FinTech is deploying AI for fraud detection and customer guidance. SMBs are leveraging AI copilots for marketing, payroll, and customer service.

The organizations that master this shift early—where human and agent collaboration becomes muscle memory—will be the ones that dominate the next decade.

The Anatomy of an Agentic Team

Think of an Agentic Team as an ecosystem with three core layers:

1. **Human Core** – The people who bring empathy, context, creativity, and judgment.
2. **Agentic Layer** – AI copilots and autonomous agents that analyze, predict, and execute.
3. **Operating Fabric** – The workflows, governance, and trust systems that bind humans and AI into a single, cohesive unit.

Let's break these down.

1. The Human Core

Humans are not going away. In fact, their role becomes even more valuable in Agentic Teams. But the kind of human talent you prioritize changes.

Instead of hiring purely for execution, you hire for **judgment, adaptability, and creativity.** The top skills shift from "can you complete this task?" to "can you guide, interpret, and redirect the AI to complete this outcome?"

Key Human Roles in Agentic Teams:

- **Orchestrators** – People who design workflows and direct agents, ensuring alignment to outcomes.
- **Sense-Makers** – People who interpret insights, weigh tradeoffs, and make judgment calls.
- **Creators** – Innovators who use AI as a multiplier for new ideas, products, and experiences.
- **Relationship Builders** – Humans who nurture trust with customers, partners, and employees in ways AI can't replicate.

Humans become the "why" and the "what." Agents increasingly own the "how."

2. The Agentic Layer

This is where AI moves from passive tool to proactive teammate.

Agentic AI isn't just "predictive analytics" or "chatbots." It's systems that can sense, decide, and act—within boundaries you set—just like a junior team member.

Roles AI Agents Play in Teams:

- **Coordinators** – Orchestrating workflows, moving tasks between people and systems.
- **Analysts** – Scanning massive data sets, spotting anomalies, surfacing patterns humans would miss.
- **Predictors** – Anticipating customer needs, risks, or outcomes before they surface.

- **Executors** – Handling repetitive actions with speed and accuracy (e.g., drafting, scheduling, responding).

The magic is in pairing human strengths (intuition, empathy, judgment) with agent strengths (scale, memory, speed).

3. The Operating Fabric

Even the best humans and the smartest AI won't gel without the right operating fabric. This is the layer where leaders often stumble.

Agentic Teams need:

- **Clear Governance** – Defining what agents can decide autonomously, what requires human oversight, and how exceptions are escalated.
- **Shared Language** – Humans and agents must "talk" in ways that are interpretable and transparent. No black-box decisions.
- **Trust Frameworks** – Both employees and customers need confidence that agents are accurate, ethical, and aligned with values.
- **Feedback Loops** – Continuous learning from outcomes, feeding back into the agent models and human decision-making.

Think of the Operating Fabric as the glue. Without it, you don't have an Agentic Team. You have chaos.

Playbook: Designing Your First Agentic Team

Here's your recipe card for building Agentic Teams in practice.

Ingredients:

- 1 bold leader willing to rethink structures
- A handful of humans strong in judgment, adaptability, and empathy
- A starter set of AI agents aligned to key workflows
- Governance and trust rules baked in from day one

Steps:

1. **Identify a friction zone.** Find a part of your business where customers or employees are feeling the most pain: onboarding delays, service tickets piling up, reporting bottlenecks.
2. **Map the human-agent split.** Break the workflow into "human strength" moments (judgment calls, empathy) and "agent strength" moments (data crunching, repetitive tasks).
3. **Deploy agents as teammates, not tools.** Introduce agents into the workflow with a role title, like "Onboarding Coordinator" or "Customer Health Analyst." Frame them as team members, not software.
4. **Establish governance.** Decide: what can the agent do without human approval? When should it escalate? How does it log decisions?

5. **Measure both efficiency and experience.** Track not just time saved, but also customer satisfaction, employee relief, and trust in the agent.
6. **Iterate and expand.** Once the first Agentic Team shows results, replicate the model in other functions. Scale horizontally.

Common Pitfalls to Avoid

1. **Treating AI as "set and forget."** Agents need coaching, feedback, and retraining—just like humans.
2. **Failing to invest in human skills.** If employees aren't trained to orchestrate and sense-make, they'll feel threatened instead of empowered.
3. **Over-automation.** Not every interaction should be agentic. Use humans where it matters most.
4. **Ignoring culture.** Agentic Teams aren't just about tech. They're about building a culture where people trust and value their AI teammates.

Culture: The Hidden Superpower

Let's talk culture.

Agentic Teams thrive when the culture shifts from "humans vs machines" to **"humans + machines."**

That requires leaders to model the behavior. When a manager introduces an AI agent in a team meeting as "our new teammate EVA," and thanks EVA for compiling insights overnight, it sets the tone.

It also requires psychological safety. Employees must feel safe experimenting, asking dumb questions, and admitting when the agent got it wrong.

The organizations that win won't just deploy more AI. They'll build cultures where human-agent collaboration feels natural, trusted, and even fun.

Future State: The Fluid Organization

Imagine what this looks like five years out.

- A marketing team where AI agents dynamically reallocate budget based on campaign performance in real time, while humans focus on storytelling and brand.
- A sales team where agents qualify leads, predict churn risk, and handle initial outreach, while humans nurture high-value relationships.
- A product team where AI agents analyze user behavior, propose new features, and even generate prototypes, while humans decide direction and customer experience tradeoffs.

The org chart itself becomes fluid. Teams assemble dynamically around problems, with humans and agents pulling in and out as needed. Hierarchies give way to **networks of collaboration.**

That's the true promise of Agentic Teams.

From Fear to Empowerment

Every big shift comes with fear. Employees will ask: "Will I be replaced?" Leaders will wonder: "Can we trust the AI?" Customers may worry: "Am I talking to a machine?"

Your job as a leader is to flip fear into empowerment.

- Show employees how agents free them from drudgery.
- Show leaders how agents give them sharper foresight.
- Show customers how agents create faster, more personal experiences.

This isn't about replacing humans. It's about releasing them into higher levels of impact.

Closing Thought: Build the Orchestra

If I leave you with one metaphor, it's this:

An Agentic Team is like an orchestra. The humans are the composers, conductors, and soloists. The AI agents are the rhythm section, the strings, the horns—the instruments that create scale, depth, and precision.

Without humans, you get noise. Without agents, you get limitations. Together, you get music.

Your job as a leader is to build that orchestra. To design organizations where humans and AI collaborate seamlessly, not just co-exist. To create a future where every teammate—human or agent—plays their part in harmony.

That's how you build an Agentic Team. And that's how you future-proof your business.

"Collaboration runs on data—the lifeblood of agency. In the next chapter, we'll turn data from a static asset into a living, breathing system."

CHAPTER 8

Data as a Living Asset

Agentic transformation only works if data is clean, accessible, and actionable.

The Day the Dashboard Lied

It started with a celebration.

A CEO stared at a glowing dashboard—95% customer health. Green across the board. The team clapped, investors smiled, and everyone believed the story that the data told.

But beneath the glossy charts, something was wrong. Churn was climbing. Renewals were slipping. And the AI models—trained on this same "healthy" data—were confidently suggesting the wrong actions.

When they finally uncovered the truth, it was too late. The data was polluted—duplicates, stale entries, missing context. The dashboard hadn't lied. It had told the story exactly as it was instructed to.

That's the hidden danger of transformation in the age of AI: **dirty data disguised as intelligence.** It looks polished. It sounds automated. But it quietly erodes trust, decisions, and growth.

This is where many organizations fail—not because their AI isn't smart enough, but because the data feeding it isn't alive.

From Static to Living Data

"Data is the new oil."
— Clive Humby

"Information is the oil of the 21st century."
— Peter Sondergaard

We've heard these metaphors for years. But oil gets drilled, refined, and burned once. Data doesn't. Data multiplies. It learns. It evolves.

In this new era, data isn't just something you *store*—it's something you *steward*. It breathes through every system, product, and decision. It feeds your agents and learns from every interaction.

If automation was the muscle of transformation, data is the bloodstream. And when the bloodstream clogs, the whole system fails.

The most adaptive organizations today treat their data like a living organism—constantly sensing, updating, and self-correcting. Every signal matters. Every loop teaches. Every connection strengthens the intelligence of the enterprise.

Static data is a snapshot. Living data is a heartbeat.

Truth and Trust

"Garbage in, garbage out" isn't just a cliché—it's a modern-day business threat.

When a spreadsheet is wrong, a few bad decisions happen.

When an AI model is wrong, **thousands** of bad decisions happen automatically.

Agentic systems amplify everything: precision or error, fairness or bias. A mislabeled customer record triggers the wrong marketing campaign. A biased dataset hardwires discrimination. A duplicate record distorts your renewal rates and erodes executive confidence.

Ronald Coase once said, "Torture the data, and it will confess." He was right—but in the AI age, it might confess to the wrong crime.

This isn't a technology problem. It's a truth problem.

Because you can't build superintelligence on half-truths.

Data as Currency

For small and mid-sized businesses, data is the most undervalued asset they own.

You wouldn't leave $100,000 in an unlocked drawer—but that's exactly what happens when companies ignore their CRM hygiene, feedback systems, or analytics pipelines.

Every customer interaction, every invoice, every chat log is a deposit in your "data bank." But just like money, data depreciates if it sits idle. It must circulate—through analytics, systems, and feedback loops—to create value.

Carly Fiorina said it perfectly: "The goal is to turn data into information, and information into insight."

That's the difference between survival and scale.

The businesses that will thrive in this decade won't be the ones with the biggest budgets. They'll be the ones with the cleanest, most connected, and most trusted data ecosystems.

Data for Everyone

Data trapped in executive dashboards is dead. Data that flows across every team is alive.

A marketer tweaking campaigns.

A customer success manager predicting churn.

A product lead deciding which feature to build next.

A CEO making a bet on the next market.

All of them should be powered by the same living truth.

Stephen Few once wrote, "Numbers have an important story to tell." But they can't speak if they're locked away.

When data becomes accessible, contextual, and conversational, it changes the culture. Teams stop guessing and start designing decisions together. Alignment becomes natural. Trust becomes measurable. And every person becomes part of the intelligence loop.

How AI Learns to Think

AI doesn't get smarter through code—it gets smarter through feedback.

Every click, every anomaly, every success or failure becomes new input. A customer responds to an outreach? That's data. A product feature flops? That's data too. Every moment your system observes becomes a micro-lesson for your agents.

That's what keeps intelligence alive—the constant exchange between human judgment and machine learning.

When the loop breaks, AI grows arrogant—confident but wrong.

When the loop stays active, AI grows adaptive—humble, self-correcting, and continuously improving.

That's the real magic of agentic systems. They don't just follow instructions. They evolve through experience.

From Data Chaos to Data Consciousness

Data consciousness begins with a mindset shift:

Yesterday	Tomorrow.
Data is stored	Data flows
Reports are delivered	Insights are discovered
Governance restricts	Governance guides
Dashboards summarize.	Agents interpret
Data belongs to IT	Data belongs to everyone

It's not about dashboards—it's about dialogue.

Humans and systems learning together, with shared context and mutual trust.

Your agents can't act intelligently if they're starved of signal.

Your people can't act confidently if they don't trust the numbers.

When both are aligned, intelligence becomes cultural, not technical.

The Playbook for Living Data

Step 1: Audit for Health, Not Volume.

Trace where your data comes from, how it moves, and where it decays. Clean before you automate—or you'll just scale the mess.

Step 2: Connect Everything.

Build a unified data fabric that links Sales, CS, Product, and Finance. Everyone should operate from one source of truth.

Step 3: Make Data Conversational.

Deploy AI copilots or chat-based dashboards so anyone can ask questions in plain language and act instantly.

Step 4: Close the Feedback Loop.

Every action or outcome should flow back into the system. Every success, every loss—each one sharpens intelligence.

Step 5: Measure Trust, Not Just Volume.

The real metric isn't terabytes—it's confidence. Do your teams believe the data enough to act fast?

Start Simple

Merge duplicate records.

Automate nightly cleaning jobs.

Launch a #data-insights Slack channel.

Run a weekly "Data Friday" to share one action taken from an insight.

Add a chatbot to your workspace that lets anyone ask, *"What's churn by region this quarter?"*

Small steps compound. Trust builds. Intelligence accelerates.

Closing: Data as DNA

Data doesn't just describe your business—it defines it.

It encodes your values, decisions, and behaviors. It's the memory and the mirror of your organization.

The smartest leaders don't see data as a system—they see it as the **DNA of superintelligence.**

They don't hoard it. They nurture it.

They don't just collect it. They connect it.

And they don't just look at it—they learn from it, continuously.

Because in the end, intelligence doesn't rise from algorithms—it rises from the quality of the data that fuels them:

clean, connected, and alive.

That's when transformation stops being digital—and starts becoming agentic.

🪏 Recipe Card: The Living Data Framework

Turn Chaos into Clarity and Build the Foundation for Agentic Intelligence

Outcome

A living, breathing data ecosystem that fuels intelligent decisions, enables AI agents, and builds organizational trust.

⏱ Time to Run

Phase 1 setup: 4–6 weeks

Continuous optimization: Ongoing

Core Insight

Data doesn't just describe your business—it *drives* it.

When data flows freely and feeds back continuously, every agent, every team, and every decision gets smarter over time.

Ingredients

- Clean source data from CRM, ERP, CS, and Finance systems
- API or integration layer (Zapier, Snowflake, Databricks, or equivalent)
- AI copilot or data chatbot (ChatGPT, Power BI Copilot, or Tableau Pulse)
- Governance checklist (privacy, bias, accuracy)

- Executive sponsor + cross-functional data stewards
- Defined metrics for trust, accuracy, and utilization

Preparation (Step-by-Step Playbook)

Step 1: Map the Data Flow

→ Trace how data enters, moves, and decays across your organization.

→ Label every key source (CRM, product, support, marketing, finance).

→ Identify duplicates, blind spots, or "dark data" that never gets used.

Step 2: Clean Before You Connect

→ Apply a "trust first" rule: clean, validate, and normalize data before automation.

→ Build quality gates to flag incomplete or inconsistent entries.

→ Remember: agentic AI magnifies both insight and error.

Step 3: Build a Living Data Fabric

→ Integrate systems so data flows bidirectionally.

→ Replace static reports with connected dashboards that refresh automatically.

→ Adopt metadata tagging so agents understand data context, not just content.

Step 4: Democratize Access

→ Give every function (Sales, CS, Product, Finance) the ability to query data through AI copilots or natural language dashboards.

→ Train teams to ask better questions, not just request more charts.

Step 5: Design Feedback Loops

→ Feed user actions and outcomes back into your data lake or AI model.

→ Example: when a customer renews after a campaign, tag it as success data for the next predictive cycle.

→ Keep the data ecosystem learning.

Step 6: Measure and Monitor

→ Track trust as a key metric: how many teams use the data confidently and act on it.

→ Audit monthly for drift, bias, or decay.

→ Publish data "health scores" just like financial KPIs.

Quick Wins

1. De-duplicate customer and account data—start with CRM and billing.
2. Launch a "Data Confidence Dashboard" showing accuracy % and gaps.
3. Create a single Slack or Teams channel for live metrics + anomaly alerts.

4. Use ChatGPT or Copilot to let anyone query: "Show me churn trends by segment this quarter."

Who Benefits

- **Executives:** Confident, data-backed decisions.
- **Customer Success:** Accurate health scores and proactive plays.
- **Marketing:** Smarter segmentation and ROI tracking.
- **Product Teams:** Real feedback shaping roadmap.
- **Finance:** Unified view of revenue truth.

Signature Insight

Data is not an asset you own—it's a living ecosystem you *steward*. Nurture it, circulate it, and let it learn.

Because in the age of super intelligence, **your data doesn't just reflect reality—it creates it.**

"Once data becomes intelligent, growth becomes orchestration. Let's explore how to conduct adoption, retention, and expansion like a symphony."

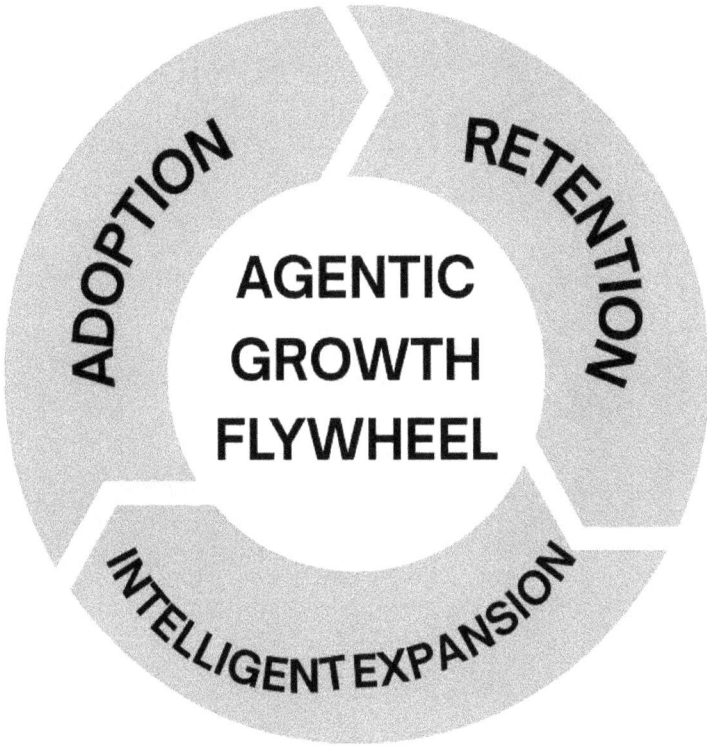

Agentic Growth FlyWheel

CHAPTER 9

Orchestrating Growth

Adoption, Retention, and Intelligent Expansion as the New Growth Playbook

---

"Growth and comfort do not coexist."

— Ginni Rometty

The old growth playbook is dead.

It was built for a world of endless budgets, predictable customers, and linear funnels. That world no longer exists.

Today, growth isn't a straight line—it's a living system. The winners aren't the ones who sell the fastest. They're the ones who orchestrate harmony between **adoption, retention, and intelligent expansion**—powered by data, trust, and agentic AI.

This isn't "customer success." This is *customer symphony.*

From Funnels to Flywheels

Once upon a time, growth meant hunting. Land a deal. Move on. Repeat.

But the funnel mindset created exhaustion. Teams chased logos instead of loyalty, numbers instead of outcomes. Companies bled customers as fast as they won them.

Agentic enterprises are rewriting the score. Growth today starts *after* the sale—when customers use, love, and expand what you deliver.

It's not acquisition-led anymore. It's **adoption-led, retention-fueled, and expansion-intelligent.**

1. Adoption: Turning Promise into Proof

"Customers don't measure you on how hard you tried. They measure you on what you deliver."
— Steve Jobs

Adoption is the first moment of truth. It's where excitement meets execution.

In the old world, onboarding was a sprint: train them, send docs, check a box.

In the new world, adoption is a dialogue: listen, personalize, adapt in real time.

Agentic adoption is powered by intelligent systems that learn from every action.

They don't just teach customers *what* to do—they show them *why it matters*.

Imagine an onboarding bot that adjusts content based on behavior.

Imagine predictive nudges that detect disengagement and re-engage automatically.

Imagine day two value, not day sixty.

That's adoption reimagined—not a checklist, but a first win.

2. Retention: Earning the Right to Stay

"Retention is the new growth."

— Brian Balfour

Retention isn't about preventing churn—it's about earning trust repeatedly.

Agentic retention systems turn raw data into living insights. They sense friction early, connect signals across usage, sentiment, and business value, and trigger the right play at the right time.

No more annual "renewal panic." No more "let's wait and see."

Retention becomes the bass line of your business—steady, rhythmic, and essential.

AI doesn't replace the CSM; it amplifies them. It whispers, *"This customer is at risk. Here's why. Here's what to do."*

The best retention strategies don't chase customers—they *reassure* them that staying is the smartest move.

3. Intelligent Expansion: Growth Without Friction

> *"Revenue is vanity. Profit is sanity. Cash is king."*
> — Alan Miltz

Expansion used to feel like sales pressure. Now it feels like alignment.

The new era of growth is *intelligent expansion*—powered by context and timing.

AI agents read the room before you enter it. They know when a customer's value curve is peaking and when an additional product, feature, or service would multiply impact—not add clutter.

Expansion isn't about pushing more. It's about enabling *more of what works*.

When done right, customers see upgrades not as spend—but as scale.

4. The Orchestra Effect

"Every company is now a software company."
— Satya Nadella

Growth is no longer linear—it's orchestral. Adoption plays the melody. Retention keeps the rhythm. Expansion hits the crescendo.

When connected by AI, these elements stop being departments and start being movements.

Marketing, sales, success, and product share one intelligence fabric—data flowing freely, insights looping continuously, feedback feeding strategy.

The result?

A business that doesn't chase growth—it *conducts* it.

The Orchestrated Growth Flywheel

Here's how it flows:

- **Adoption sparks value.** Customers see results early.
- **Value drives retention.** They stay and advocate.
- **Retention builds trust.** That trust opens the door.
- **Trust enables expansion.** Growth compounds organically.

Agentic AI keeps the flywheel spinning—predicting risk, identifying opportunity, and nudging teams toward action before humans even notice the trendline shifting.

It's not automation. It's orchestration at scale.

The Playbook: How to Orchestrate Growth

Step 1: Start with Outcomes, Not Onboarding.

Make day-one success visible. Tie every early action to a measurable result.

Step 2: Instrument Continuous Listening.

Deploy AI to monitor sentiment, usage, and business signals—every day, not every quarter.

Step 3: Automate Micro-Value Moments.

Celebrate wins automatically: "You saved 22 hours this month." Small signals build loyalty.

Step 4: Predict Renewal Risk Early.

Don't wait for red flags. Let your AI co-pilot surface "weak signals" before humans sense them.

Step 5: Guide Expansion Intelligently.

Trigger contextual offers when usage maturity peaks—not when your quota does.

Step 6: Align the Orchestra.

Sales, CS, and Product should run from one shared intelligence layer. No silos. No ego. Just harmony.

Why This Matters

The companies winning right now—whether SaaS, FinTech, or SMB—aren't growing because they have bigger sales teams. They're growing because they have *smarter orchestration engines.*

They've moved from chasing growth to designing it.

Agentic systems are not replacing humans—they're freeing them.

Freeing leaders to think strategically.

Freeing teams to build relationships.

Freeing customers to experience progress, not paperwork.

The Rise of Intelligent Growth

"Growth and comfort do not coexist."
— Ginni Rometty

Growth used to be an outcome.

Now, it's an ecosystem—alive, adaptive, intelligent.

And just like an orchestra, the magic isn't in one instrument.

It's in how they play together.

When AI conducts the rhythm and humans bring the soul, growth stops being accidental—it becomes *inevitable*.

Key Takeaway

Growth in the agentic era isn't a funnel—it's a flywheel.

Adoption drives retention. Retention powers expansion. Expansion reignites adoption.

The faster the wheel spins, the less force it needs.

Your role?

Don't chase the music. Conduct it.

"Even the best playbooks fail in the wrong culture. To truly scale intelligence, we must first upgrade the human operating system—culture itself."

GROWTH ORCHESTRA

Retention

Adoption

Expansion

CHAPTER 10

Culture as the Operating System

Why Culture Determines Whether AI Adoption Succeeds or Fails

The Invisible Force That Decides Everything

"Culture is what people do when no one is looking."

— Herb Kelleher

When we talk about technology transformation, especially one as seismic as artificial intelligence, the conversation too often collapses into tools, platforms, and features.

- *Which vendor should we pick?*
- *What model is more accurate?*
- *How do we integrate AI into our workflows?*

These are valid questions, but here's the truth: none of them matter if the underlying culture of the organization isn't aligned.

Culture is the operating system of a business. It is the invisible code that determines how decisions get made, how risks are taken (or avoided), how people collaborate (or don't), and how fast an organization can adapt. You can implement the most advanced AI platform in the world, but if your culture rejects it, buries it in bureaucracy, or reduces it to a shiny pilot project that never scales, you've accomplished nothing.

AI doesn't fail because the math was wrong. It fails because the culture wasn't ready.

And on the flip side, when the culture is right—curious, adaptive, inclusive, bold—AI adoption becomes not just possible but inevitable. It becomes part of the DNA of how the business operates.

That's what we're going to unpack in this chapter.

Why Culture Eats AI for Breakfast

Peter Drucker famously said, *"Culture eats strategy for breakfast."* In the era of AI, I'll push that further: culture eats AI for breakfast, lunch, and dinner.

Why? Because AI adoption isn't only about technology—it's about trust, experimentation, and mindset.

Let's break this down:

1. **Trust in Machines, Trust in People** AI introduces a new decision-making partner into the room: algorithms. If your culture doesn't trust data, doesn't trust its leaders, or doesn't trust itself, how will it ever trust a machine?
2. **Experimentation vs. Perfectionism** AI thrives in iteration. You test, you learn, you refine. A culture addicted to perfection and allergic to failure will never allow AI to grow roots.
3. **Speed vs. Paralysis** The AI landscape moves at breakneck speed. Cultures that debate endlessly, hoard information, or demand five layers of approval simply can't keep pace.
4. **Inclusivity vs. Gatekeeping** AI isn't just for data scientists. It's for frontline workers, customer success managers, marketers, HR leaders. If your culture excludes, the adoption will stall. If your culture democratizes, the adoption will soar.

In other words: culture is the multiplier. It determines whether AI is a force-multiplier or a money pit.

The Hidden Resistance Points

"Fear has no place in innovation."
— Satya Nadella

Every leader loves to claim, *"Our culture is innovative. We embrace change."* Yet when you look closer, the hidden resistance points emerge.

- **Fear of job loss.** People whisper: *"Will AI replace me?"*
- **Middle management bottlenecks.** Leaders who protect fiefdoms block new workflows.
- **Lack of psychological safety.** Employees don't feel safe experimenting or raising concerns about AI outputs.
- **Old reward systems.** People are still rewarded for the number of hours worked, not the outcomes achieved.
- **Ethics theater.** Companies put on panels about AI ethics but never embed accountability in daily operations.

If you don't address these, AI adoption will become surface-level—an experiment in one department that never scales.

Culture as the Operating System: A Playbook

So how do you design culture to be the OS that allows AI to thrive? Here's the playbook I've seen work in companies that successfully scale adoption.

"The way to right wrongs is to turn the light of truth upon them."
— Ida B. Wells

Step 1: Establish a North Star Narrative

AI adoption isn't just about efficiency. It's about empowerment. Craft a clear story that connects AI to the mission of your company.

- *"AI will free our people from repetitive tasks so they can spend more time with customers."*
- *"AI will help us spot risks earlier, protect our brand, and serve our communities better."*

Narratives matter. People need to understand the "why," not just the "what."

Step 2. Create Psychological Safety

No one will experiment with AI if they fear being punished for mistakes. Leaders must model curiosity, admit when they don't know something, and celebrate learning over perfection.

Practical move: Celebrate "best failed experiment" each quarter. Make it visible.

Step 3: Redesign Incentives and Metrics

If you reward only "keeping the machine running," don't be surprised when people avoid AI experiments that might disrupt workflows. Update incentives to include learning, innovation, and customer impact.

Practical move: Tie performance reviews to adoption milestones (e.g., "how did you use AI to improve your work?").

Step 4: Democratize Access

AI cannot be the secret toy of one innovation lab. Put tools in the hands of everyone. Create "AI fluency" programs for every role, not just technical teams.

Practical move: Launch a monthly AI showcase where employees present real use cases they've tried.

Step 5: Build Guardrails, Not Walls

Yes, AI carries risks. But building walls ("no AI allowed!") paralyzes innovation. Instead, set clear guardrails (ethical principles, data privacy guidelines) and empower teams to operate freely within them.

Practical move: Publish a 1-page "AI Principles" doc that everyone can understand.

Step 6: Lead with Transparency

Admit the limits of AI. Share openly when models are biased, when outputs are wrong, and how you're addressing it. A transparent culture builds trust faster than a perfect one.

Case Study: Two Companies, Two Outcomes

Let's make this concrete.

Company A: The Fear Culture

This company announced an "AI-first" initiative with big fanfare. But inside, managers whispered that jobs might be cut. The innovation team hoarded tools. Employees who tried ChatGPT were scolded for "shadow IT." Incentives still awarded the number of hours worked, not the impact of new tools.

Result? Three years later, they're still stuck as pilots. Their "AI program" is little more than a marketing line.

Company B: The Empowerment Culture

This company started small: a North Star narrative about AI freeing humans for higher-value work. They trained everyone, from frontline workers to executives, on basic AI literacy. They launched "AI Fridays" where teams showcased experiments. They set clear guardrails and celebrated bold attempts—even failed ones.

Result? Within 18 months, AI was embedded in customer service, finance, HR, and product. Their employee satisfaction scores rose because people felt empowered, not threatened.

The difference wasn't the technology. It was the culture.

The CEO as Chief Culture Hacker

"Change before you have to."
— Jack Welch

AI adoption is not an IT project. It's a CEO-level mandate. The leader's role is to act as the chief culture hacker—constantly reinforcing behaviors that enable AI to thrive.

This means:

- Talking about AI in every town hall.
- Rewarding leaders who share learnings.
- Calling out when old cultural habits (gatekeeping, fear, perfectionism) creep back in.

A leader who says, *"We are an AI-powered company, and that means we are a learning-powered company,"* sets the tone for everyone else.

Culture Shifts That Enable AI

Here's the shift map I use with executive teams:

It's a rewiring. And just like rewiring an operating system, it takes both technical upgrades (tools) and human upgrades (mindset).

The Agentic Culture

Let's bring this back to the book's central theme: agency.

An agentic culture is one where humans and AI collaborate seamlessly. Where individuals don't wait for permission to try AI tools but are empowered to experiment responsibly. Where teams view AI not as a threat but as a teammate.

In an agentic culture:

- AI is not a tool on the side; it's woven into how strategy, execution, and learning happen.
- Humans are not cogs; they are empowered to make decisions faster with AI's help.
- Leaders don't cling to control; they expand control by distributing intelligence across the system.

This is what separates organizations that thrive in the AI age from those that fade.

The Cultural Operating System Checklist

If you're a leader reading this, here's your practical checklist to know whether your culture is ready for AI:

- Do employees trust leadership to use AI responsibly?
- Do they feel safe experimenting with AI, even if it fails?
- Are incentives aligned to reward adoption and outcomes?
- Does every employee, regardless of role, have access to AI tools?

- Are ethical guardrails clear and simple?
- Is transparency practiced, not just promised?
- Is the CEO personally championing AI as both a technology and cultural shift?

If you can check most of these, your culture is the right OS. If not, your AI adoption will stall.

Closing: The Hard Truth

Here's the hard truth: AI doesn't transform organizations. Culture does. AI is simply the accelerant.

Think of it like fire. In a culture soaked in fear, bureaucracy, and mistrust, AI is gasoline on dysfunction—it makes the problems worse. But in a culture built on trust, learning, and empowerment, AI is gasoline on innovation—it ignites progress at scale.

Culture is the operating system. AI is just the application. And like any application, it can only run as well as the OS allows.

So as you think about your AI journey, don't just ask: *"Which tool should we buy?"* Ask: *"What culture are we running?"*

Because the future of AI adoption will not be written in code. It will be written in culture.

CULTURE SHIFTS THAT ENABLE AI

OLD CULTURE	NEW CULTURE FOR AI
Fear of replacement	Confidence in augmentation
Perfection before release	Iteration and learning
Top-down decisions	Inclusive experimentation
Hoarding data	Radical transparemcy
Rewarding effort	Rewarding outcomes
Walls of compliance	Guardrails of trust

Culture Shifts

"Culture creates leaders—and leaders, in turn, shape culture. Next, we'll define the traits of those who can lead fearlessly in the AI age."

CHAPTER 11

The Future Leader

The Mindset and Behaviors Leaders Must Embody in the AI Era

"A leader is one who knows the way, goes the way, and shows the way."
— John Maxwell

Every era of transformation produces a new archetype of leader.

The industrial era gave us operational commanders.

The digital era elevated analytical builders.

The AI era demands something entirely different: **future leaders who are fluent in both humanity and intelligence—leaders who can harness machines while elevating people.**

Let me be clear—AI is not replacing leaders.

It's exposing them.

In boardrooms, startups, and scale-ups across industries, leaders who cling to yesterday's playbook are already being outpaced by those willing to unlearn, relearn, and lean into the unknown. This chapter is about what it takes to be that kind of leader—the ones who don't just survive in the AI era but define it.

Why the Old Model of Leadership is Breaking

For decades, leadership was about control and certainty. The boss had the answers. Information was power. Hierarchies were clear. Success was about optimization—squeezing more efficiency out of the same system.

That model cracks in the face of AI.

AI systems don't just optimize but they reinvent. Information isn't locked in leadership offices—it flows freely across digital platforms. The leader who tries to control everything becomes the bottleneck. The one who claims to "know it all" becomes irrelevant the moment an algorithm surfaces insights faster.

The leaders of the future will not be defined by **how much they know**, but by **how well they guide, connect, and design systems that scale beyond them.**

The Future Leader's Operating Mindset

"Innovation is the ability to see change as
an opportunity, not a threat."
— Steve Jobs

Mindset is everything. It's the operating system of leadership. In the AI era, there are five core mindsets that separate future leaders from obsolete ones.

1. Explorer's Mindset: Comfort with Ambiguity

Future leaders treat uncertainty not as a threat but as their natural habitat. They move forward without needing the full map. They experiment, test, and pivot. They understand that AI adoption isn't a linear project plan—it's a winding path with detours and discoveries.

Behavioral Shift: Instead of "I'll decide once I know everything," the future leader says, "I'll decide once I know enough to test—and I'll adjust as we learn."

2. Augmentation over Replacement

Old-school managers look at AI and think: "What jobs will it cut?"

Future leaders ask: "How will it make my people more powerful?"

They see AI as an **exoskeleton, not a guillotine.** It extends human capacity, amplifies creativity, and removes friction. Their role isn't to strip teams down, but to reimagine what humans can do when freed from the mundane.

Behavioral Shift: They reward people not for resisting AI but for co-creating with it. They ask every employee: *"What task do you hate that AI could take off your plate?"*

3. Systems Thinker's Lens

Future leaders don't just manage departments; they design ecosystems. They understand that in the AI era, value is created at the intersections—between humans and machines, data and intuition, automation and empathy.

They zoom out, see patterns, and design feedback loops. They don't get stuck on tools; they architect operating models.

Behavioral Shift: In every decision, they ask, *"How does this change ripple through the whole system?"*

4. Bias Detector and Trust Builder

AI exposes us to biases—because it learns from us. A future leader doesn't blindly trust AI outputs. They interrogate them. They put guardrails in place. They create cultures where questioning the algorithm is not rebellion but responsibility.

Trust becomes their true currency—trust with customers, employees, and society. Without it, AI adoption fails.

Behavioral Shift: They don't just say, *"The AI said so."* They say, *"Here's why we trust or challenge the AI's recommendation."*

5. Humanity as the Differentiator

Here's something to consider: the more intelligent machines become, the more valuable our humanity gets. Empathy, storytelling, vision, and creativity aren't "soft skills"—they are the differentiators.

Future leaders don't outsource their humanity to AI; they double down on it. They become architects of belonging, meaning, and purpose. They lead not just with metrics but with mission.

Behavioral Shift: They prioritize conversations that can't be automated—moments of listening, encouragement, and inspiration.

The New Leadership Behaviors

Mindset without behavior is just aspiration. Future leaders operationalize their mindset into daily behaviors. These are not lofty theories; they are visible practices people can feel in the room.

1. Transparency as Default

In the AI era, secrecy backfires. Teams expect to know how decisions are made, how algorithms are trained, and what data is used. Future leaders model radical transparency—sharing not just outcomes, but reasoning and trade-offs.

Practice: Hold AI "explainability sessions" where leaders walk teams through how a decision or output was reached. Make it normal for employees to challenge the logic.

2. Micro-Learning, Macro-Adaptation

Future leaders know learning isn't a workshop once a year. It's micro-bursts embedded into daily work. They encourage teams to experiment with new AI tools, share quick demos, and cross-train.

Practice: Replace quarterly "training" with weekly "AI use case show-and-tells." Keep the learning loop alive.

3. Inclusion by Design

AI can exclude if left unchecked. Future leaders hardwire inclusion into design. They ensure diverse voices shape training data. They invite cross-functional teams into problem-solving. They measure not just performance, but equity of impact.

Practice: In every AI initiative, ask: *"Whose voice is missing in this decision? Whose experience might be left out by this design?"*

4. Speed + Stewardship

Yes, future leaders move fast. But they also hold the steering wheel responsibly. They balance urgency with ethics. They don't get seduced by shiny tools; they anchor adoption in real human outcomes.

Practice: Before rolling out an AI tool, leaders run a two-question check:

1. Does this accelerate value?
2. Does this protect trust?

Both must be yes.

5. Presence in the Age of Distraction

AI automates communication. Notifications never stop. The temptation is to lead through dashboards and messages. Future leaders know nothing replaces presence. They show up—in person or virtually—with attention fully on their people.

Practice: Block "AI-free hours" where leaders engage only with humans. No dashboards. No automation. Just people.

The Leader's Playbook: From Boss to Orchestrator

"The function of leadership is to produce more leaders,
not more followers."
— Ralph Nader

The future leader is less like a general commanding troops and more like a conductor orchestrating a symphony. Each instrument—human or machine—has its role. The magic is in the coordination.

Here's a practical playbook:

Step 1: Set the Score (Vision): Define the "why" clearly. People and machines need the same north star.

Step 2: Assign Instruments (Roles): Humans play empathy, creativity, judgment. AI plays pattern recognition, automation, prediction.

Step 3: Conduct with Rhythm (Pacing): Know when to push fast and when to slow down for alignment.

Step 4: Listen for Harmony (Feedback): Constantly tune the system. If one section drowns out another, rebalance.

Step 5: Elevate the Soloists (Empowerment): Spotlight individuals who experiment, take risks, and show what's possible.

The leader doesn't play every instrument—they make sure the music works.

Common Traps for Today's Leaders

If the future leader sounds aspirational, let's ground it in the pitfalls that keep many stuck in yesterday.

1. **Tool Worship:** Leaders confuse buying AI tools with leading transformation. AI is not a tool problem—it's a culture and leadership problem.
2. **Control Reflex:** They cling to being the smartest person in the room. In the AI era, the smartest room is the one connected to AI.
3. **Short-Termism:** They chase cost cuts instead of building long-term capabilities. Efficiency without vision becomes a race to the bottom.
4. **Exclusion:** They let only technical teams shape AI strategy. That creates blind spots, ethical risks, and adoption failure.
5. **Silence:** They avoid hard conversations about bias, job shifts, and ethics. Silence kills trust faster than mistakes.

Future leaders name the elephants, invite voices in, and keep moving.

"Management is about arranging and telling. Leadership is about nurturing and enhancing."

— Tom Peters

The Future Leader's Compass

Let's distill everything into a compass—four directions to guide leadership in the AI era:

- **North: Purpose.** Anchor every decision in why you exist. AI amplifies what you aim it at. Make sure the target is meaningful.
- **East: People.** Remember: technology is nothing without human adoption, creativity, and trust.
- **South: Systems.** Design beyond silos. Think ecosystems, feedback loops, and scalability.
- **West: Stewardship.** Guardrails, ethics, inclusion—don't move fast and break trust.

This compass ensures leaders never get lost, no matter how fast the landscape shifts.

Closing Call: The Leaders We Need

The AI era doesn't just need executives. It needs **future leaders—** individuals who are explorers, orchestrators, and guardians of trust. Leaders who know that AI adoption succeeds not because of the tools, but because of the culture, systems, and behaviors they model.

This chapter isn't a prediction. It's a manifesto.

Because the truth is, leadership in the AI era is not about learning how to manage machines. It's about learning how to unlock the **best in people while shaping a future where humans and intelligence rise together.**

And if you're reading this, that future leader might just be you.

Purpose
Anchor every decision
in why you exist

People
Remember:
technology
is nothing
without
human
adoption,
creativity,
and trust

Stewardship
Guardrails,
ethics, inclusion—
don't move fast
and break trust

Systems
Design beyond silos.
Think ecosystems,
feedback loops,
and scalability

"The future leader's final act is design. In the next chapter, we'll build the full blueprint of an Agentic Enterprise—resilient, intelligent, and customer-obsessed."

CHAPTER 12

Designing the Agentic Enterprise

A blueprint for building resilient, intelligent, and customer-obsessed enterprises

From Fragile Systems to Living Enterprises

Every decade, business leaders declare they've "reinvented" the enterprise. We've seen waves of total quality management, digital transformation, cloud adoption, agile frameworks, and customer-centric movements. Yet underneath, most organizations still operate on brittle systems, fragmented silos, and manual decision chains that break under pressure.

The pandemic exposed this fragility. Supply chains snapped. Customer service queues ballooned. Growth strategies stalled. Most companies responded with band-aids: more dashboards, more Zoom calls, more middle-management oversight. But the truth is simple: the operating model itself was outdated.

Enter the **Agentic Enterprise.**

An enterprise designed not as a machine of rigid processes, but as a living, learning organism—one that senses, adapts, and grows. Agentic Enterprises don't just survive disruption; they harness it. They are resilient because they're intelligent at the core. And they're customer-obsessed not as a tagline, but as the natural consequence of how they operate.

This chapter is a blueprint. It's not theory. It's a practical design for leaders who want to build organizations where **human creativity and AI agency work in concert**—a model that delivers durable growth, customer trust, and future-proof agility.

The Core DNA of an Agentic Enterprise

Think of the enterprise as an organism. Like any living system, it must have DNA—a code that dictates how it grows and adapts. For the Agentic Enterprise, this DNA rests on three strands:

1. **Resilience** – The ability to bend without breaking, to recover faster, and to adapt at speed.
2. **Intelligence** – Not just having data, but embedding predictive and generative intelligence into every decision and workflow.
3. **Customer Obsession** – Designing every process, policy, and product around the customer's evolving journey.

Without resilience, the enterprise crumbles in crisis.

Without intelligence, it drowns in complexity.

Without customer obsession, it becomes irrelevant.

These three strands intertwine, reinforced by AI agents that act as connective tissue across the enterprise.

Principle 1: Resilience as a Design Choice

Resilience isn't luck. It's an architectural choice.

Traditional organizations optimize for efficiency—squeezing out every ounce of cost, streamlining processes until there's no buffer. The problem? That's like building a bridge with no flex. It looks sleek until the first earthquake.

Resilient enterprises design for optionality. They embrace **redundancy, scenario planning, and distributed decision-making**. AI amplifies this by running simulations, stress-testing strategies, and dynamically reallocating resources.

Playbook Moves for Resilience

- **Digital twins** of supply chains and operations to model shocks before they happen.
- **Agentic monitoring** that detects anomalies in customer experience, employee engagement, or financial performance in real time.
- **Adaptive workforce systems** where AI agents match talent supply to demand surges, preventing burnout.
- **Decentralized decision rights**, supported by AI advisors, empowering teams to act fast without waiting for top-down approvals.

Resilience is the muscle memory of the Agentic Enterprise. It ensures that when the unexpected strikes, the organization doesn't freeze; it flexes.

Principle 2: Intelligence Everywhere

Enterprises have long chased "single sources of truth." They centralize data lakes, build BI dashboards, and hold endless "data strategy" meetings. The irony? By the time leaders get the report, the opportunity has passed.

Agentic Enterprises reject passive data. Instead, they deploy **intelligence everywhere**—embedding AI agents directly into processes, so decisions are informed and adaptive in the moment.

Examples of Intelligence in Action:

- A **sales AI co-pilot** that listens to calls, identifies buying signals, and nudges reps in real time.
- A **finance agent** that forecasts cash flow scenarios daily, not quarterly.
- An **HR agent** that predicts attrition risk weeks before resignation letters land.
- A **customer journey agent** that stitches signals across email, chat, product usage, and billing to anticipate churn and trigger retention plays.

The shift is profound. Intelligence moves from being a "destination" (a dashboard you log into) to being **ambient** (always present, always assisting).

This doesn't eliminate human judgment. It elevates it. Humans decide with context, nuance, and ethics—AI accelerates the pattern recognition, freeing leaders from analysis paralysis.

Principle 3: Customer Obsession as the Operating North Star

Most companies say they're customer-centric. Few actually are. They measure NPS once a quarter, send out a survey, or add "customer first" to a poster.

In the Agentic Enterprise, **customer obsession is systemic**. Every agent, every workflow, every OKR or KPI aligns with one question: *Does this create more value for the customer?*

Blueprint for Customer Obsession:

- **Agentic CX orchestration**: Predictive agents that don't just react to issues but anticipate needs before customers articulate them.
- **Personalization at scale**: Content, pricing, product experiences tuned to each customer's context, powered by dynamic AI profiles.
- **Feedback loops that learn**: Every interaction—complaint, compliment, click—is fed back into the enterprise brain, closing the loop in hours, not quarters.
- **Customer-inspired innovation**: R&D pipelines that prioritize ideas validated by real customer behaviors, not just executive hunches.

Customer obsession is not a department. It's the gravitational force that keeps the entire enterprise aligned.

The Architecture of the Agentic Enterprise

Now, let's get concrete. What does the architecture of an Agentic Enterprise look like?

Picture four interlocking layers:

1. **Agentic Core** – The AI agents, orchestration layer, and governance framework that power intelligence and automation.
2. **Adaptive Processes** – Workflows designed for change, not rigidity. Processes modular enough to reconfigure as needs shift.
3. **Empowered People** – Humans trained, incentivized, and trusted to co-create with AI. Roles redesigned to maximize creativity and empathy.
4. **Customer Gravity** – A system of metrics, rituals, and incentives that keep the customer at the center.

Each layer reinforces the others. Agents don't replace people; they amplify them. Processes aren't rigid SOPs; they're living playbooks. Customers aren't endpoints; they're co-architects of value.

Designing the Enterprise Playbook

To build the Agentic Enterprise, leaders need more than inspiration. They need a playbook—a sequence of moves that translate ambition into architecture.

Here's a blueprint:

Step 1: Diagnose the Current State

- Map where fragility exists—broken processes, slow decision cycles, siloed data.
- Identify where intelligence already flows and where it bottlenecks.
- Audit customer experience from outside-in, not inside-out.

Step 2: Define the Agentic North Star

- Craft a clear narrative: "We are building an enterprise that is resilient, intelligent, and customer-obsessed."
- Anchor this vision in both cultural language and operational metrics.

Step 3: Deploy Agentic Pilots

- Choose high-impact domains—customer success, sales, supply chain.
- Deploy AI agents to augment humans in these areas.
- Measure not just cost savings, but speed, quality, and customer outcomes.

Step 4: Scale with Governance

- Create an **Agentic Operating Framework**: ethics guardrails, data security, human oversight.
- Ensure cross-functional alignment—IT, HR, Finance, Operations—so adoption doesn't stall in silos.

Step 5: Institutionalize Customer Obsession

- Redesign incentives—tie bonuses and promotions to customer outcomes, not internal metrics.
- Establish **customer obsession councils** where frontline insights inform strategic bets.
- Bake customer signals into daily operating rhythms, not quarterly reviews.

Step 6: Build Continuous Learning Loops

- Treat every AI model, every process, every initiative as a living experiment.
- Close the loop fast: test, learn, adapt, redeploy.
- Use AI to monitor adoption and identify friction.

The playbook isn't linear. It's iterative, compounding over time. Each step strengthens resilience, deepens intelligence, and tightens customer focus.

Human Roles in the Agentic Enterprise

There's fear that AI will erase human roles. The opposite is true—if we design correctly.

In Agentic Enterprises, **human creativity, judgment, and empathy** become even more valuable. AI absorbs the drudgery. Humans focus on the high-order work machines can't replicate.

Evolving Human Roles:

- **Decision Orchestrators** – Leaders who interpret AI insights and align them with ethics, context, and strategy.
- **Customer Advocates** – Humans who translate customer emotion into enterprise action.
- **Innovation Catalysts** – Employees freed from repetitive tasks to experiment, prototype, and imagine.
- **Trust Builders** – Individuals who ensure transparency, communicate AI use, and reinforce confidence with customers.

Rather than eliminating jobs, the Agentic Enterprise redefines them. Work becomes less about bandwidth, more about impact.

The Culture That Sustains It

Technology can't compensate for toxic culture. Even the smartest AI agents fail in organizations ruled by fear, hierarchy, or inertia.

That's why culture isn't just important—it's the **operating system**. The Agentic Enterprise thrives on cultures that are:

- **Experimental**: failure is feedback, not a career-ending event.
- **Transparent**: AI decisions are explainable, not black boxes.
- **Collaborative**: cross-functional teams share ownership of outcomes.
- **Obsessively Customer-Driven**: customer stories, not just metrics, guide decisions.

Without this cultural foundation, the blueprint collapses. With it, enterprises unlock compounding advantage.

A Glimpse Into the Future Agentic Enterprise

Let's imagine:

A customer logs into a digital platform. An agent recognizes not just who they are, but their intent—based on patterns across thousands of signals. Instead of generic menus, the platform presents tailored actions: an upgrade offer timed to their budget cycle, support content aligned to a recent behavior, and a proactive nudge that resolves an issue before it surfaces.

Behind the scenes, AI agents coordinate across finance, operations, and service. If the customer accepts the upgrade, billing, provisioning, and onboarding trigger automatically. A human CSM reviews, adds a personal note, and schedules a value-add call.

The entire journey feels seamless, almost invisible. The enterprise doesn't feel like a faceless machine. It feels like a trusted partner that anticipates, adapts, and personalizes at scale.

That's the Agentic Enterprise in motion. Not science fiction. Just good design.

Closing: Building for the Era Ahead

The question is not whether enterprises will adopt AI. That ship has sailed. The real question is: *Will they adopt it in a way that makes them resilient, intelligent, and customer-obsessed—or will they slap AI on top of broken systems and call it transformation?*

The winners of the AI era will be those who design differently. Who understand that resilience is built, not assumed. That intelligence must be ambient, not siloed. That customer obsession is not marketing, but operating truth.

The Agentic Enterprise is not a buzzword. It's the next blueprint for business. A living, learning, customer-anchored organism that thrives in disruption and compounds advantage over time.

Leaders who embrace this blueprint will do more than modernize. They will future-proof. They will earn the right to serve customers not just today, but in the decades ahead.

And in doing so, they'll prove the ultimate truth:

Enterprises don't fail because of technology gaps. They fail because they weren't designed to be agentic.

The future belongs to those who choose to design.

THE 4 LAYERS OF THE AGENTIC ENTERPRISE

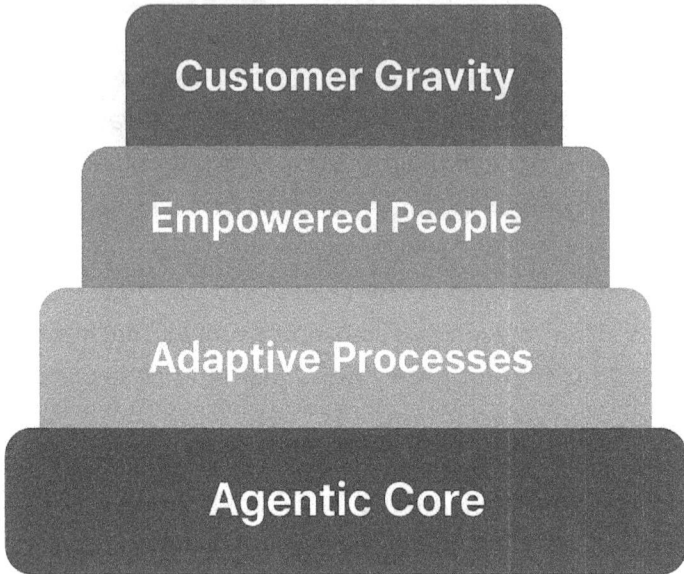

Customer Gravity

Empowered People

Adaptive Processes

Agentic Core

"Theory only matters if it turns into action. The following recipes translate every idea in this book into ready-to-run playbooks."

THE RECIPE LIBRARY

Ready to use Playbooks

Welcome to Your Agentic Kitchen

Most business books give you frameworks. This one gives you **recipes**.

Think about it: when you buy a cookbook, you're not looking for the history of carrots. You want something you can make tonight. Same here.

These recipes are **ready-to-use playbooks** for the agentic era. No waiting. No excuses. You'll walk away from this chapter with at least one agent running on your behalf before you go to bed.

Every recipe follows the same rhythm:

- **Name & Outcome:** What you'll get out of it.
- **Time to Run:** How long to go from zero to working.
- **Ingredients:** The accounts, connectors, and context you need.

- **Steps:** A simple flow you can follow without being "technical."
- **Prompt Starters:** Copy, paste, and run.
- **Quality Check:** How to know if it worked.
- **Metrics:** How to measure impact.

Think of them like your **AI mise en place: organized,** everything prepped, no clutter, no guesswork.

▨ Recipe 1: Connect ChatGPT to Gmail & Calendar

Outcome: ChatGPT "sees" your inbox and schedule so you never have to copy-paste again.

Time to Run: 15 minutes.

[Subscribe for Full recipe text]

Story Beat:

When I first connected Gmail + Calendar, I felt like I had a silent chief of staff. Suddenly, my Monday morning prep took five minutes instead of fifty.

▨ Recipe 2: Email Triage & Reply Agent

Outcome: Achieve inbox zero without stress.

Time to Run: 20 minutes.

[Subscribe for Full recipe text]

Story Beat:

A VP of Sales once told me: *"I spend two hours a day on email. That's half a workweek every month."* After using this agent, he reclaimed **40 hours/month**. That's a workweek he now spends closing deals, not clearing threads.

▨ Recipe 3: Newsletter Machine

Outcome: Turn weekly chaos into a polished digest.

Time to Run: 30 minutes/week.

[Subscribe for Full recipe text]

Story Beat:

I tested this recipe with a small SaaS founder. Before, his newsletter took him four hours. After, it took thirty minutes. He said: *"This feels like cheating... in the best way."*

▨ Recipe 4: Onboarding Agent

Outcome: Every new customer feels cared for from Day 1.

Time to Run: 45 minutes setup, then autopilot.

[Subscribe for Full recipe text]

Story Beat:

One Customer Success Manager I worked with was drowning in 20 onboardings at once. After building this agent, she ran all 20 on the same framework, without missing a detail. Her manager said: *"This is the first time onboarding hasn't been chaos."*

▨ Recipe 5: CS Playbook Generator

Outcome: Create a full-blown Customer Success playbook on demand.

Time to Run: 20 minutes.

[Subscribe for Full recipe text]

Story Beat:

This recipe is my secret weapon. In workshops, I've had entire teams build adoption, expansion, and renewal plays in one afternoon. Normally, that takes a quarter.

1

SETTING UP CHATGPT AND CONNECTING TO GMAIL, CALENDAR, ETC.

Getting Chat-GPT ready for action is easier than you think! Follow these steps to configure it and link it to various services

RECIPE

TITLE
ChatGPT Setup

SKILL LEVEL
Beginner

INGREDIENTS
- Create an acount on the ChatGPT platform
- Set up and configure API keys

INSTRUCTIONS
1. Create an account on the ChatGPT platform
2. Set up and configure API-keys
3. Use ChatGPT to link to Gmail, calendar, etc.

2

CREATING AN EMAIL AGENT OR PROMPT

Crafting an email agent is a piece of cake! Check out the following steps to make one that drives results

RECIPE

TITLE
Email Agent

SKILL LEVEL
Easy

INGREDIENTS
- ChatGPT
- Email data

INSTRUCTIONS
1. Develop ChatGPT prompt for the email agent.
2. Provide relevant email data for context.
3. Test the agent to refine its performance
4. Put the email agent into action!

Email Triage & Reply Agent

Outcome: Inbox zero without stress

✓ Ingredients

✓ Gmail connector turned on

✓ Your preferred email voice (casual, exec, consultant)

Time to Run:
20 minutes/day

Connect Gmail → **Paste Prompt** → **Review Drafts**

```
You are my Email Triage Assistant.
Goals: (1) Prioritize inbox, (2)
Extract actions,
(3) Draft concise replies in my
voice: (insert tome).
From Gnail, summarize unread emails
today + urgent / important / low:
For each urgent or importantthread:
draft a reply (120 words max.)
```

50%
less time
in inbox

25+
Emails cleared/
session

Inbox
Zero achieved
daily

✓ Quality Check

✓ Correct urgent vs. low-priority classification

✓ Draft replies sound like YOU

✓ No sensitive info mishandled

♀ Pro Tip
Paste 3 of your past emails so the agent learns your tone.

⚠ Watch Out
Always review drafts.

③ CREATING A NEWSLETTER PROMPT

Want to churn out engaging newsletters in a snap? A ChatGPT-powered prompt can help you write fresh and relevant content in no time—here's how.

RECIPE

TITLE
Newsletter Prompt

SKILL LEVEL
Easy

INGREDIENTS
- Audience details
- Topics
- Key points

INSTRUCTIONS
1. In ChatGPT, write a prompt like. "Create an engaging newsletter for [audience] about [topics], highlight kie𝒗𝒚]
2. Review the content generated and make any adjustments.
3. Send it out or schedule it for later.

3

CREATING A NEWSLETTER PROMPT

Building a newsletter prompt is simple as can be Just follow these steps:

RECIPE

TITLE
Newsletter Prompt

SKILL LEVEL
Easy

INGREDIENTS
- ChatGPT
- Topic details

INSTRUCTIONS
1. Compose a ChatGPT prompt for generating newsletter content.
2. Include important details about the topic.
3. Test out the prompt and adjust as needed
4, Generate the newsletter with ChatGPT

ONBOARDING AGENT

★ ★   ★ ★

RECIPE

YIELD: ONBOARDING ASSISTANT

INGREDIENTS

- System prompt for onboarding
- List of tasks for role setup
- Desired tone and style

DIRECTIONS

1. Write a system mesaage for onboarding new hires.

2. Prepare a series of onboarding tasks, providing clear instructions and explanations.

3. Specify the tone and style the agent should use in interactions.

4. Deploy the onboarding agent and test its performance

🍳 Recipe 5

CS Playbook Generator

Outcome: One prompt → full CS playbook PDF draft

🕐 **Time to Run:**
20 minutes

✅ **Quality Check**

✓ Playbook sections genera fully

✓ Messaging is professional, not generic

✓ Metrics are measurable, not fluffy

✅ **Ingredients**

✓ ChatGPT + your ICP context

✓ Optional: templates in Knowledge

```
You are a Customer Success Playbook Generator.
Output structure:
  : Purpose & When to Use
  : Ideal Customer Profile
  : 3 Plays (Adoption, Exp. Expansion, Renewal)
  : Cadence: 0-30-60-90
  : Messaging Library
  : Risk Triggers & Saves
  : Metrics
  : Roles & RACI
Add 10-line "First Run" script.
Return in Markdown with checkboxes.
```

12

# of playbooks generated

4 hrs

Time saved per playbook

100+

Adoption/expansion outcomes

📖 FinTch's AI Inflection Point
Transforming Trust, Risk & Growth with Agentic AI

🍔 Core Ingredients (What You Need)
- Agentic AI Frameworks — dynamic, self-otymizaiinì sistcmsrawware
- Trust Signals — belanod, self-optimisly bun (beyonrd credit scores)
- Risk Simulation Engines — predictive models running what *Iff* sca-
- Compllance & Governannce Protocols — ethics, fairness, trans.
- Human Expertise

🧑 Preparation (How to Build)
1. Recode Trust → Move from generic scaiv → *hyp*-pearalizàtice → hyde tha "AI decisions mode → "hwiieer-decisions
2. Shift Risk Managemant → continuous predictive simuladatiċns.» → factor in macro signals with *"cootus* → preemptive símula-
4. Build Ethical Guardrails → bake transprarncency: aradis-
5. Keep Humans in the Loop → Keep humans in the Loop

⚡ Quick Wins (Immediate Moves)
- Deploy AI-driven fraud shields · Pilot AI-powerd micro-lending
- Automate compllance with regiutatory agents emderᴏ

🌐 Serving Suggestions (Who Benefits)
- Banks & Credit Unions   · SMBs & Startups
- Investors & Wealth Managers   Incesu⌄rs & Wealth Managers

💡 Signature Insight
FinTech's inflection point isn't about faster transactions..It's about programmable trust, predictive risk, and transformational growth. The winners will be those who balance AI's intelligence with human empathy.

The Age of Intelligent Reinvention

We have reached a point in human history where intelligence is no longer a fixed trait, but it is a **co-created force**. Every algorithm, every agent, every system we build is, in truth, a mirror of who we are becoming.

For decades, we've trained machines to think like us. Now, we must learn to **lead like them,** adaptive, curious, ever-evolving, while keeping the **soul of humanity** intact.

The rise of *SuperIntelligence* isn't a story about technology.

It's a story about **us, it is** about courage in uncertainty, creativity in constraint, and consciousness in motion.

Businesses that once scaled through efficiency will now scale through **intelligence**.

Leaders who once commanded through control will now inspire through **clarity and connection**.

And individuals who once feared automation will discover that the most powerful automation begins with **alignment** of purpose, data, and human intent.

It's the intelligence that sees customers as co-creators, teams as ecosystems, and data as living energy that fuels transformation.

To lead in this era is to bridge two worlds:

> the rational precision of AI and the irrational beauty of human imagination.

When those worlds merge, growth becomes exponential, not just in profits, but in purpose too.

So as you close this book, pause for a moment.

And recognize that the next chapter isn't written here — it's written **through you.**

Because the real transformation is not happening in cloud servers or neural nets.

It's happening in every conversation, every decision, every act of creation that chooses alignment over automation, and intelligence over impulse.

You don't have to wait for the future to arrive.

You are already in it.

And it's rising — through you, with you, and because of you.

Rise. Build. Lead.

This is the Age of Intelligent Reinvention.

This is ***SuperIntelligence Rising***.

EPILOGUE

The Phoenix Principle

There's a moment that comes after every storm.

When the noise fades. When the smoke clears. When you stand in the stillness and realize—you didn't just survive. You transformed.

That moment is what I call The Phoenix Principle.

It's not a theory. It's a truth that lives in every person, every company, every system that chooses growth over grief, design over despair, and agency over fear.

It's the moment when you stop waiting for change and start becoming change.

When I began this book, I was standing in my own ashes—of career upheaval, personal heartbreak, and uncertainty. But fire, I've learned, isn't just destruction. It's purification. It burns away what no longer serves and makes space for something greater to rise.

And in that space, *Fhyris* was born—not as a company, but as a belief: That human resilience and intelligent systems are not opposites—they are extensions of one another.

That we can build enterprises that think, teams that feel, and leaders who rise higher because of AI, not despite it.

Every chapter of this book has been a blueprint for that rise:

How to turn automation into intelligence.

How to turn intelligence into agency.

How to turn agency into shared growth.

And how to turn growth into a movement that uplifts everyone connected to it.

But here's the part no one tells you—

Transformation isn't a single event. It's a cycle.

The phoenix doesn't rise once. It rises every time life demands reinvention.

You will face your own inflection points.

A market that shifts overnight.

A career that no longer fits.

A system that breaks just as you start to trust it.

And in that moment, you'll have two choices:

Cling to what was—or create what's next.

The Agentic Era isn't about machines replacing us.

It's about machines revealing what's *most human* in us—our imagination, empathy, and courage to start again.

So wherever you are reading this—from a corner office, a kitchen table, or the quiet middle of a new beginning—remember this:

- You are not behind. You are becoming.
- You are not being replaced. You are being redefined.
- And your rise is not a reaction—it's a design.

May this book serve as your compass and your spark.

Build boldly. Lead intentionally.

And when the next fire comes—and it will—

walk through it with open eyes.

Because the world doesn't need more survivors.

It needs more phoenixes.

It needs you.

Welcome to your rise.

Welcome to the Rise of Super Intelligence — not artificial, but beautifully human.

🩶 *Rajitha Rupani*

AFTERWORD

The Rise Ahead

We've reached the edge of the map.

The end of the old playbooks.

The beginning of something audacious, that is a future we don't inherit, but co-create.

Every chapter of this book has been a blueprint for what comes next — not just for business, but for humanity. The story of *SuperIntelligence Rising* isn't about machines replacing people. It's about people remembering who we are — creators, designers, orchestrators of possibility, finally building systems that think *with* us, not *for* us.

AI is now everywhere, diffused, democratized, and amplifying every dreamer with the courage to act. The question is no longer, "Will AI take my place?"

The real question should be, "What will I do with the intelligence now at my fingertips?"

We stand at a crossroads between fear and design. Between automation and agency.

Between a world optimized for profit and one optimized for potential.

What happens next depends on whether we lead with intention.

Because intelligence without purpose is chaos — but intelligence guided by values, empathy, and vision becomes creation itself.

This is the call to rise, not as users of technology, but as co-architects of the intelligent era. To build enterprises that think like ecosystems, to design leaders who are fluent in both data and humanity, to raise a generation that sees AI not as magic, but as a mirror reflecting the best of what we can become.

We have the chance to write a new social contract between humans and machines, the one where ethics are built into algorithms, creativity sits beside computation, and dignity is woven into design.

💜 *Rajitha Rupani*

BONUS CHAPTER

Real Estate Reinvented

The AI Playbook for Realtors and Property Managers

Real estate has always been about location.

Now, it's about **intelligence.**

The most successful Realtors and property managers aren't just selling homes — they're orchestrating data, automation, and AI agents that think faster than markets shift. From prospecting to property maintenance, every step can now be predicted, personalized, and automated — freeing agents to focus on relationships, not repetitive tasks.

The AI Shift

Traditional real estate ran on hustle. Modern real estate runs on **hybrid intelligence:**

- Predictive models forecast neighborhood appreciation and rental yields.

- AI copilots draft listings, contracts, and offers in minutes.
- Chatbots nurture leads 24/7 while you sleep.
- Smart sensors and maintenance agents flag issues before tenants call.

What once took ten humans now takes one — guided by AI precision.

The Realtor's Agentic Playbook

Step 1: Prospect Intelligently

→ Use AI lead scorers (like BoomTown or ChatGPT-trained CRMs) to identify high-conversion prospects.
→ Automate your outreach cadence with contextual scripts that learn from engagement.

Step 2: Predict Market Moves

→ Leverage predictive analytics (Reonomy, Zillow API, or local MLS data) to identify undervalued properties.
→ Build your own "AI comp engine" that adjusts pricing dynamically based on trends.

Step 3: Automate the Mundane

→ Draft listings, emails, and contracts with generative AI.
→ Use voice-to-text tools for field notes that instantly sync with your CRM.

Step 4: Create Living Property Portfolios

→ For property managers, use IoT + AI maintenance systems to predict HVAC, plumbing, or energy issues.

→ Enable tenant AI portals that handle 80% of requests autonomously.

Step 5: Build the Digital Twin

→ Each property becomes a digital replica: performance dashboards, energy consumption, tenant sentiment, and predictive maintenance in one view.

Result:

You go from agent → orchestrator.

From managing listings → managing intelligence.

From commission checks → compound growth.

"In the Agentic Era, Realtors don't chase leads — their AI agents attract, qualify, and close them."

Real Estate Reinvented
The AI Playbook for Realtors & Property Managers

🧠 CORE INSIGHT

Real estate no longer runs on hustle alone—it runs on **hybrid intelligence**. AI now automates lead generation, predicts market frends, writes listings, and even manages tenant relationships. The future Realtor isn't a salesperson —they're a–strategic orchestrator of intelligent ecosystems.

⚡ OUICK WINS

- Use ChatGPT to rewrite property listings for emotional appeal & SEO
- Automate your showing schedule with AI-powered calendar sync
- Launch a "24/7 Tenant Concierge" chatbot
- Track portfolio ROI using AI-driven dashboards

🍊 SERVING SUGGESTIONS

- Realtors → More closings. less chasing
- Property Managers → Predictive maintenance, happy tenants
- Investors > Faster insights, higher ROI

🏆 OUTCOME

A high-efficiency, AI-powered real estate business that runs on automation, prediction, and personalization—freeing you to focus on relationships and growh.

🫚 PREPARATION STEP-BY-STER PLAYBOOK

Step 1. Prospect Intelligently
- Use AI lead scorers to identify and rank high-probability clients.
- Automate personalized outreach sequences that learn from engagement.

Step 2. Predict Marke Moves
- Build dashboards that analyze local market trends, property appreciation, and rental yield forecasts, Let AI recommend pricing strategies and investment timing.

Step 3. Automate the Munlane
- Geherate listings, email campigns and contracts outomatically.
- Record voice notes →transcribe →auto-sync to your CRM

Svetze Digital Twins—Build a 'Iving profile" for each property with data on performance, energy use. tenant sentiment, and maintenance history,

BONUS CHAPTER

Campus to Capital

The AI Playbook for College Students

You don't need a job to start your career.

You need **agency** — the power to act, learn, and build wealth with AI as your co-founder.

Every generation had its edge — the industrialist had factories, the coder had the internet, and **you have intelligence on demand**. ChatGPT, Claude, Midjourney, ElevenLabs, Perplexity — these aren't apps; they're your first unpaid employees.

How to Think Like an AI-Era Entrepreneur

The question isn't *"What job should I apply for?"*

It's *"What problem can I solve using intelligence that scales?"*

AI has flattened the playing field. You can now:

- Build a micro-agency overnight (design, writing, automation, tutoring).
- Create digital assets that earn while you sleep.
- Use AI to find high-income skills faster than any class ever could.

The Agentic Student Playbook

Step 1: Define Your Edge

→ Pick a domain you understand (fitness, gaming, real estate, fashion).

→ Ask AI: "What problems do people in this niche pay to solve?"

Step 2: Train Your Digital Co-Founder

→ Create a custom GPT or agent that helps you deliver your service: design prompts, write pitches, or manage leads.

Step 3: Launch Micro

→ Sell your first digital service on Fiverr, LinkedIn, or Upwork.

→ Automate delivery using AI templates and workflows.

Step 4: Learn, Earn, Repeat

→ Track results → refine → automate → scale.

→ Turn every project into a case study — employers or investors love proof of execution.

Step 5: Build Your Personal Brand

→ Post your learnings weekly on LinkedIn or TikTok using AI tools for content.

→ Visibility creates opportunity — jobs and investors now find *you*.

Optional Track: The Fast-Track to Income

- Start a micro-agency: "AI-Powered Marketing for Local Businesses."
- Build a niche GPT: "College Resume Coach" or "Real Estate Listing Writer."
- Create a monetized Notion template or eBook with AI-generated assets.

"In this age, you're not competing for jobs — you're competing for intelligence. Whoever learns to *deploy* it fastest wins."

GET RICH .GPT

The AI Playbook for College Students

🧠 CORE INSIGHT

Forget flipping burgers—start flipping the game. AI can be your co-founder, marketer, coach, and investment researcher all rolled into one. Whether it's launching a startup or securing that dream job, your secret weapon is coded intelligence—not coined experience.

⚙ INGREDIENTS

- ChatGPT or similar AI chatbot
- AI writing tools
- AI no-code app builders
- AI design & marketing platforms

⚡ QUICK WINS

- Launch a simple website with your*AI*site.builder
- Prompt ChatGPT to write a business plan or cover letter
- Grow a niche audience with AI-curated content.
- Analyzer assets with an AI investment copilot

🧩 OUTCOME

Financial independence and career acceleration by using AI to start a business, secure a high-value position, and sidestep the traditional grind.

✒ PREPARATION

I STEP-BY-STEP PLAYVK

- Launch ä simple website with your*AI*site.builder
- Prompt ChatGPT to write a business plan or cover letter
- Grow a niche audience with AI-curated content
- Analyzer assetta with an AI investment copilot

🍽 SERVING SUGGESTIONS

- Aspiring Founders → First revenue streams in dorm room
- Job Seekers → Personalized prep, standout applications
- Entrepreneurs → Automated. marketing, scalable ventures
- Investors → Smarter allocation, earlier independence

> "Your co-founder got a 1600 on the Digitai SAT and never*sleeps.* Why wait for real world experience—when you can generate your own."

QUICK REFERENCE GUIDE

How to Use This Index

Use this page as your **navigation system**:

- Skim chapters for inspiration.
- Jump to recipe cards for action.
- Apply the frameworks as playbooks for transformation in your own company

Your journey to SuperIntelligence starts wherever you decide to rise.

Chapter	Core Concept / Takeaway	Corresponding Recipe Card / Framework
Introduction – Rising Through Transformation	Reinvention as design. Resilience + AI as catalysts for a new era of agency.	
1. The Age of Agency	Shared agency between humans + AI as the foundation of future work.	Agency Compass – Vision / Collaboration / Values / Resilience
2. From Automation to Intelligence	Moving from rule-based automation to adaptive, learning intelligence.	Intelligence Playbook – 5 Steps from Fragile to Fluid Systems
3. The Agentic Customer	Hyper-personalization and predictive AI driving co-created experiences.	Agentic CX Playbook – 3 Levels of Predictive Experience
4. FinTech's AI Inflection Point	Programmable trust, predictive risk, and ethical finance at scale.	FinTech Recipe Card – Trust → Risk → Growth Framework
5. Healthcare Without Friction	AI agents as orchestrators of care, removing friction from the patient journey.	Frictionless Care Playbook – 7 Steps to Predictive Patient Experience
6. SMBs as Giants	Small businesses scaling globally through digital-first AI strategies.	SMB Growth Stack – Automate → Predict → Personalize → Scale
7. Building Agentic Teams	Designing organizations where humans and AI collaborate seamlessly.	Agentic Team Playbook – Human Core + Agentic Layer + Operating Fabric

Chapter	Core Concept / Takeaway	Corresponding Recipe Card / Framework
8. Data as a Living Asset	Treating data as a living, evolving system that feeds intelligence.	*Living Data Framework* – 6 Steps to Build Continuous Feedback Loops
9. Orchestrating Growth	Adoption, retention, and intelligent expansion as the new growth symphony.	*Growth Flywheel* – Adoption → Retention → Expansion
10. Culture as the Operating System	Culture as the invisible code that enables or blocks AI success.	*Cultural OS Checklist* – 7 Questions to Test AI Readiness
11. The Future Leader	Leaders as orchestrators of intelligence—balancing speed, trust, and humanity.	*Future Leader Compass* – Purpose / People / Systems / Stewardship
12. Designing the Agentic Enterprise	Blueprint for resilient, intelligent, customer-obsessed enterprises.	*Agentic Enterprise Blueprint* – 3 DNA Strands: Resilience / Intelligence / Obsession
Epilogue – The Phoenix Principle	Transformation as a cycle. Agency as rebirth. Reinvention as design.	*Phoenix Principle Framework* – Rise → Redefine → Rebuild → Reignite

Chapter	Core Concept	Playbook
1.	The Age of Agency	The Agentic Compass
2.	From Automation to Intelligence.	The Intelligence Playbook
3.	The Agentic Customer	The Empowerment Flywheel
4.	FinTech's AI Inflection Point	Programmable Trust
5.	Healthcare Without Friction	AI Care Flow System
6.	SMBs as Giants	Digital-First Scaling Blueprint
7.	Building Agentic Teams	Human-AI Collaboration Map
8.	Data as a Living Asset	Living Data Framework
9.	Orchestrating Growth	Agentic Growth Flywheel
10.	Culture as OS	Culture Reinvention Framework
11.	The Future Leader	AI-Age Leadership Traits
12.	Designing the Agentic Enterprise	The Blueprint for the Intelligent Era

www.ingramcontent.com/pod-product-compliance
Lightning Source LLC
Chambersburg PA
CBHW070927210326
41520CB00021B/6832